# Rodin

## THE CANTOR FOUNDATION GIFT TO THE NORTH CAROLINA MUSEUM OF ART



DAVID STEEL

north carolina museum of art

THIS PUBLICATION IS MADE POSSIBLE BY A GENEROUS GIFT FROM THE IRIS AND B. GERALD CANTOR FOUNDATION.

THE NORTH CAROLINA MUSEUM OF ART, LAWRENCE J. WHEELER, DIRECTOR, IS AN AGENCY OF THE NORTH CAROLINA DEPARTMENT OF CULTURAL RESOURCES, LINDA A. CARLISLE, SECRETARY. OPERATING SUPPORT IS PROVIDED THE STATE OF NORTH CAROLINA, BEVERLY EAVES PERDUE, GOVERNOR, AND GENEROUS CONTRIBUTIONS FROM INDIVIDUALS, FOUNDATIONS, AND BUSINESSES.

DESIGNER AND TYPESETTER: BARBARA WIEDEMANN
EDITOR: KAREN COCHRAN KELLY
PHOTO EDITOR: JENNIFER DASAL
PHOTOGRAPHERS: KAREN MALINOFSKI, CHRISTOPHER CICCONE

PRINTED IN CANADA

NORTH CAROLINA MUSEUM OF ART
2110 BLUE RIDGE ROAD
RALEIGH, NORTH CAROLINA 27607
WWW.NCARTMUSEUM.ORG

Library of Congress Cataloging-in-Publication Data

North Carolina Museum of Art.
Rodin : the Cantor Foundation gift to the North Carolina Museum of Art / David Steel.
p. cm.
Includes bibliographical references and index.
ISBN 978-0-88259-993-9 (hardback : alk. paper) -- ISBN 978-0-88259-994-6 (softcover : alk. paper) 1. Rodin, Auguste, 1840-1917--Catalogs. 2. Sculpture, French--19th century--Catalogs. 3. Sculpture, French--20th century--Catalogs. 4. Iris and B. Gerald Cantor Foundation--Art collections--Catalogs. 5. Sculpture--North Carolina--Raleigh--Catalogs. 6. North Carolina Museum of Art--Catalogs. I. Rodin, Auguste, 1840-1917. II. Steel, David. III. Title. IV. Title: Cantor Foundation gift to the North Carolina Museum of Art.
NB553.R7A4 2010
730.92--dc22

2010000513

FOR IRIS

## CANTOR FOUNDATION FOREWORD

In 2003 I was standing in the train station in Florence, Italy, waiting to purchase a ticket for Siena. Behind me in line were two Americans: early twenties, fresh-faced, happy. And we started to chat. They had traveled to Italy together for the summer and were awed by the sights and the art. Then we shared: "And what do you do?" When I told them I curate a private collection of Rodin sculpture, the young man became rhapsodic.

"Oh," he glowed. "A few years ago I saw the most wonderful exhibition of Rodin sculpture." He spoke to the young woman: "It was before we met." Then to me: "It was beautiful to look at, and there was so much of it. I drove from college in the next state to see it."

"Where was the show?" I asked.

"The North Carolina Museum of Art," he replied.

This was my introduction to the public impact our year 2000 exhibition *Rodin: Sculpture from the Iris and B. Gerald Cantor Collection* had on that region of the country. **In eighteen weeks 306,000 people visited the Museum. They came from all over the area**—some even from other states, like my new friends in Italy. It was obviously an unforgettable experience for them.

I had been executive director of the Iris and B. Gerald Cantor Foundation for two years and had shepherded the exhibition to Australia, Singapore, Utah, Florida, Ohio, and Iowa. Prior to its arrival in North Carolina, the exhibition had traveled to seventeen museums all over the country. These were wonderful and significant showings at some world-class museums, but none equaled the one at the North Carolina Museum of Art for public impact, beauty of installation, and significance of events.

Today I am often asked why the Foundation has chosen to give so many Rodins to the North Carolina Museum of Art. The short answer is we have long believed there should be a center to study Rodin in the southeastern United States. And the experience we had with the North Carolina Museum of Art in 2000 assured us that the very best place for such a Rodin center would be at this remarkable institution, under the inspired leadership of Lawrence J. Wheeler and the superb curatorship of David Steel.

So to my friends from the train station line in Florence, I say *grazie* for the wonderful memory you gave me. And to the North Carolina Museum of Art, heartfelt congratulations on your current achievements.

**JUDITH SOBOL** EXECUTIVE DIRECTOR, IRIS AND B. GERALD CANTOR FOUNDATION

Q Auguste Rodin, quoted in Gsell 1911, p. 136.

“The artist, in
representing the
universe as he
imagines it, formulates
his own dreams.
In nature he celebrates
his own soul. And
in doing so, he
enriches the soul
of humanity.”

## A WORD FROM IRIS CANTOR

The great French sculptor Auguste Rodin spent his life in Europe, yet his art was known and admired around the world. This widespread acknowledgment was a tribute to Rodin's genius, but it might never have continued into our time without the efforts of a select group of scholars, curators, and collectors who reintroduced his masterpieces to today's broader public.

FIG. 1: B. Gerald Cantor with *The Kiss*, New York, 1981.

Rodin's popularity and acclaim in recent decades are due in no small measure to the efforts of my late husband, B. Gerald Cantor. Bernie's "magnificent obsession" with the art of Rodin led to an extraordinary period of collecting, lending, and gifting across the United States and around the world. Sharing his appreciation for Rodin, I became his partner in this effort, and I have proudly continued his legacy through the work of the Iris and B. Gerald Cantor Foundation. Our sponsored exhibitions have attracted nearly ten million visitors, and we have furthered scholarship on Rodin at leading academic and arts institutions.

My activities on behalf of the Cantor Foundation first brought me to Raleigh in 2000, when one of our celebrated Rodin exhibitions traveled to the North Carolina Museum of Art. I will always remember both the warm welcome extended to me personally by Museum Director Lawrence J. Wheeler and his colleagues, and the phenomenal public response to the exhibition: more than three hundred thousand people visited, putting the Museum on the map with those in much larger communities.

FIG. 2: Iris and B. Gerald Cantor at Rodin's atelier (now a museum) at Meudon, outside Paris.

A few years later, when Larry and I began discussing the possibility of a major gift that would broaden the Museum's holdings to include Rodin, the exhibition's blockbuster appeal was a determining factor. It assured us that public interest would be strong. Our talks culminated in a milestone of which I am very proud: with the gifts documented in this catalogue and its accompanying DVD, the North Carolina Museum of Art has become the first museum in the southeastern United States to permanently house a major collection of Rodin sculptures.

The collection includes twenty-nine works by Rodin and one by his talented pupil Camille Claudel. Through variations in theme, physical size, and period of origin, these wondrous sculptures reflect the impressive scope of Rodin's career achievement and the significance of his work for all who behold it.

Such monumental works of art call for a distinctive setting. I am delighted the collection is housed in the new Iris and B. Gerald Cantor Court and Cantor Garden, key components of a transformative new building dedicated to the Museum's permanent collection. I am proud the Cantor Foundation gifts were a catalyst to making this vision a reality. I want to acknowledge the invaluable support of former North Carolina Governor Michael F. Easley and his wife, Mary, in achieving the Museum's ambitious goals; North Carolina cultural life has benefited immensely from their active encouragement. One of the highlights of the Cantor collection—a fifteen-inch bronze of *The Thinker*—is donated in honor of Governor Easley, for his commitment to education, and in honor of Mary Easley, in recognition of her commitment to the arts.

I am grateful to the people of Raleigh for welcoming me—and Auguste Rodin—to their beautiful city. I also extend heartfelt thanks to Larry Wheeler and the entire staff of the North Carolina Museum of Art for creating a perfect home, not only for Rodin but also for the legacies of Bernie Cantor and the Cantor Foundation.

**IRIS CANTOR** CHAIRMAN AND PRESIDENT, IRIS AND B. GERALD CANTOR FOUNDATION

## DIRECTOR'S NOTE

*"Art is the most sublime mission of mankind, since it is the expression of thought, which seeks to understand the world and to make it understood."*

AUGUSTE RODIN

Nervous, I sat in the library of the Park Avenue home of Iris Cantor, whom I had never met, to invoke her blessings on an exhibition of Rodin, which we hoped to make the most comprehensive, in terms of thematic breadth and material, ever presented in the United States. In addition to the large number of works from the Iris and B. Gerald Cantor Foundation, we hoped to include some major sculptures from the Cantors' personal collection. We also wanted her help in borrowing key works that the Foundation and she and Mr. Cantor had donated to major art museums. I came, as well, with a secret ambition to persuade Mrs. Cantor to be the honorary chair of the exhibition and the opening gala.

She joined me and immediately put me at ease. She generously agreed to all my requests and facilitated extraordinary loans from many sources. At the gala to celebrate the exhibition opening on April 29, 2000, we danced. Iris was resplendent in a sapphire blue gown by Galanos, set off by radiant sapphires and diamonds. The weekend was a festival of southern hospitality and international savoir faire. And Iris Cantor became my friend.

Over the next several years, I visited Iris in New York, Bel Air, and Palm Beach. During our ongoing, engaging conversations, we discussed her plans for the eventual disposition of the Foundation's collection. As she had when her husband was alive, she wanted the Foundation to donate sculpture to museums in the United States, particularly those that had shown Rodin with great success in their communities.

I wrote to Iris suggesting a landmark gift to the North Carolina Museum of Art, which was in the process of planning a magnificent new building to house its permanent collection. The new pavilion could include a beautiful large gallery and garden for a significant collection of Rodin sculpture. The collection would be used as a resource for neighboring universities and become a significant regional art destination. Curator David Steel and I found a shared vision of Rodin in North Carolina with our friend Iris.

In 2005 Iris Cantor announced a gift of twenty-two Rodin sculptures, and a portrait of Rodin by his muse Camille Claudel, to the North Carolina Museum of Art. **Subsequently the gift has grown to thirty sculptures and features key works from all phases of Rodin's creative career.** In April 2010 they were unveiled in the Iris and B. Gerald Cantor Sculpture Court and Garden.

My deep affection, admiration, and heartfelt appreciation go to Iris Cantor for her remarkable legacy to the citizens of North Carolina, one that will forever enrich the lives and lift the spirits of visitors to the Museum. My friendship with Iris continually stirs my heart and spreads a broad smile across my face.

To you, Iris, we dedicate this book and the accompanying documentary.

**LAWRENCE J. WHEELER** DIRECTOR, NORTH CAROLINA MUSEUM OF ART

Q Gsell 1911, p. 9.

## PREFACE

This book catalogues the generous gift of thirty sculptures—twenty-nine by Auguste Rodin and one by Camille Claudel—donated to the North Carolina Museum of Art by the Iris and B. Gerald Cantor Foundation. These works have been beautifully installed in the Iris and B. Gerald Cantor Court and Cantor Garden in the Museum's new West Building, designed by Thomas Phifer and Partners in collaboration with landscape architect Walter Havener, which opened to the public in April 2010. The accompanying DVD, created by Emmy Award–winning producer-director Art Howard and coproduced by Julie Dixon, includes professional and personal reflections on the sculptures from individuals who have been intimately involved with the collection and its donation to the NCMA. It also offers a behind-the-scenes look at the multifaceted efforts that have gone into the installation and presentation of these works at the Museum.

This book is intended to provide a useful introduction to the sculptures included in the gift. When possible, I have sought to include quotations by Rodin and his contemporaries in order to suggest how these works were viewed at the time of their creation. Because they are so familiar to us today, it is easy to lose sight of how innovative, how revolutionary, they were in their own time. Rodin's conception of sculpture and his creative process were radically different from those of any sculptor before him. **It is not enough merely to call him the first modern sculptor; he *transformed* the art of sculpture.** The words of Rodin and artists, critics, and writers of his day provide a context for understanding the transformation he brought about and a century-old lens through which we may view his works afresh.

For most of Rodin's artistic career, his sculpture received the attention of insightful critical reviewers, both favorable and hostile. We are fortunate to have the artist's own views and pronouncements concerning his approach to art, and he has been the subject of more scholarly writing, during his lifetime and over the ensuing ninety-odd years since his death, than any artist of his generation. It has been my great pleasure to learn from the scholars who have devoted many years to studying the artist and looking carefully at his creations. First and foremost of these is Albert Elsen, whose enduring friendship with Mr. and Mrs. Cantor influenced the great collection they assembled and the foundation they established. Over nearly forty years, Dr. Elsen produced an outstanding body of scholarship on Rodin, culminating in the catalogue of the magnificent collection donated by the Cantor Foundation to Stanford University. Elsen's French counterpart is Antoinette Le Normand-Romain, author of numerous studies on Rodin, the most important of which is the two-volume catalogue of Rodin's bronzes at the Musée Rodin in Paris (2007). Alongside these two authors' works, mention must be made of John Tancock's pioneering

catalogue of the collection in the Rodin Museum in Philadelphia, Leo Steinberg's perceptive essay on Rodin, and Catherine Lampert's excellent exhibition catalogue on Rodin's sculpture and drawings. Filled with insightful observations on his works, Ruth Butler's biography of the artist is the most thorough study of Rodin's life. These seminal contributions to the study of Rodin and others are listed in the Selected Bibliography.

This book and the presentation of Rodin's works in the new Museum galleries represent the combined efforts of many individuals and colleagues. It is a pleasure to acknowledge the role of Iris Cantor and the Cantor Foundation and its Board of Trustees, who understood the impact these sculptures would have on the Museum, its visitors, and the citizens of North Carolina. Their abiding, generous support has made possible this publication and the accompanying DVD. In addition to the sculptures, the Foundation donated numerous publications—essentially a library of Rodin scholarship—which greatly facilitated the research for this book and will serve as a resource for future scholars. The staff at the Cantor Foundation—in particular Executive Director Judith Sobol, Collections Manager Sheryl Nakano, and her predecessor, Jennifer Garpner—have been a delight to work with, providing wise counsel and vital assistance in handling the manifold details involved in producing this catalogue and in selecting and transporting the works to Raleigh. Many thanks also go to Allison Akbay at the Cantor Center for Visual Arts at Stanford, whose good cheer and timely responses to each of our photographic requests greatly assisted the compiling of illustrations.

My colleagues at the North Carolina Museum of Art have all done their usual superlative jobs in bringing about this book and the beautiful installation of these works. Barbara Wiedemann, associate director of publications, is responsible for the innovative design of the book and has been a constant source of support, encouragement, and ideas over the entire course of the project. The efforts of librarians Natalia Lonchyna and Patricia Stack greatly facilitated my research. John W. Coffey patiently read the earliest draft of the manuscript and made several editorial improvements. Bernard Barryte, curator of European art at the Iris and B. Gerald Cantor Center for Visual Arts, Stanford University, also read the manuscript and offered numerous helpful suggestions. Caroline Rocheleau assisted with the translation of some of the particularly challenging writings of Rodin's contemporaries. Karen Kelly greatly improved the book through her sensitive editing of the final manuscript. Jennifer Dasal provided invaluable assistance in keeping the project on track and acquiring images for comparative illustrations. Bill Brown, Stacey Kirby,

A. Rodin

Perry Hurt, Noelle Ocon, David Beaudin, and Nancy Allred, with the expert assistance of the Cantor Foundation's consultant conservator Maureen Russell, did an exemplary job examining and treating every one of the sculptures. Anyone familiar with photographing sculpture (particularly bronze sculpture) knows how daunting a challenge it presents, one that is only rarely overcome. The sumptuous and illuminating photographs that adorn these pages are the work of skilled staff photographers Karen Malinofski and Christopher Ciccone.

The outstanding presentation of these sculptures in the new Museum galleries and garden specially designed to showcase them likewise reflects the combined efforts of numerous colleagues and departments in the Museum. Chief Registrar Maggie Gregory and her staff—Marcia Erickson, Michael Klauke, William Holloman, Tom Lopez, Lee Wells, and Drew Robertson—coordinated all of the myriad details in bringing the works to Raleigh and installing them in the galleries and gardens. The elegant installation of the works is due in large measure to the efforts of Shannon Harris, Virginia Patterson, Eric Gaard, and Dan Gottlieb. My gratitude is also due to my colleagues Jenny Crow, Kathy Molesky, Sonya Robinson, and Caterri Woodrum for their assistance in various capacities. Joseph M. Bryan, Jr.; Lynne and Mark Hammerschlag; and Megan Mulder, special collections librarian at the Z. Smith Reynolds Library, Wake Forest University, generously allowed me to reproduce works from their collections. My thanks also go to the staff of Quail Ridge Books in Raleigh.

I would like to acknowledge two individuals in particular. More than anyone else, save Iris Cantor herself, NCMA Director Larry Wheeler deserves recognition for securing this extraordinary gift for the people of North Carolina. And to my wife, Daryl, go my heartfelt thanks for her patience, care, and support during the writing of this book.

My *professional* involvement with Rodin's art dates back to the late 1990s, when I first learned of the Cantor Foundation's mission to bring Rodin's works to museum audiences across America. It was then I first worked with the Foundation on an exhibition of sculpture from its magnificent collection. But my initial encounter with Rodin took place much earlier. As a fourteen-year-old, I read Robert Heinlein's *Stranger in a Strange Land* and was intrigued by his description of Rodin's *She Who Was the Helmet Maker's Beautiful Wife* and *Fallen Caryatid with a Stone* (FIG. 3). Heinlein's account inspired me to make a pilgrimage to the Rodin Museum in Philadelphia, the first art museum I had ever visited. Even in my teenage ignorance, I sensed something in Rodin's works that spoke to me in a mysterious, powerful language. I'm still listening.

**DAVID STEEL** CURATOR OF EUROPEAN ART, NORTH CAROLINA MUSEUM OF ART

FIG. 3: Auguste Rodin,
*Fallen Caryatid with Stone*,
CAT. 7.

*"Sculpture has never been held in less esteem than now. Sculptors suffer far more than painters from the autocracy of the jury. A group in plaster, a statue in marble, where can one show these? To whom can they be sold?… Not only does the jury kill poetic impulse, it is ruining our poor French artists."*

THÉOPHILE THORÉ

## INTRODUCTION

In his review of the 1846 Salon, the annual exhibition of contemporary art in Paris, the poet and art critic Charles Baudelaire sought to explain "why sculpture is boring." In his opinion sculpture compared unfavorably to painting, which he felt was more forceful. Sculpture had declined steadily since the early years of the century, largely because of its dependence on forms and subjects from classical antiquity, filtered through the art academies, where the curriculum was based on the assumption there was a single ideal style. For Baudelaire the idealized mythological figures exhibited at the Salons, though technically accomplished, were little more than monotonous echoes of a tradition that had lost its vitality and no longer held meaning for the contemporary viewer. Focusing on James Pradier, one of the reigning sculptors of the day, Baudelaire wrote, "Proof of the pitiable state of sculpture today is the fact than Mons. Pradier is its king… His talent is cold and academic. He has spent his life fattening up a small stock of antique torsos and equipping them with the coiffures of kept women… It is true that the great tradition has been lost, and that the new one is not yet established."[1] Young artists were compelled to express themselves uniformly, since it was nearly impossible to develop a successful career without access to the patronage offered through the academies of art and the annual juried Salon exhibitions.

The decadent, rote state of contemporary sculpture persisted long after 1846. Twenty-three years later, Paul Mantz offered this explanation: "What is this? Ten young men born at different times in this France where the irregularities of local temperament are still so strong: they are unequal in intelligence as well as in emotions. But they go to the same *école*, and thanks to the mechanism of an equivalent education, they transform themselves, they sweeten the spice of their individual characters, and finally end up producing identical works, absolutely the way young draftees learn to keep in step and do their exercises as a perfect ensemble."[2] It would be nearly forty years after Baudelaire's essay appeared before the tired, academic style that had dominated Western art for more than a century would begin to undergo radical transformation, and a new tradition in sculpture would emerge. Auguste Rodin would become the most dynamic agent of this transformation.

FIG. 4: Unknown photographer, Auguste Rodin, 1880, albumen print, Musée Rodin, Paris, Ph. 311.

FIG. 5: James Pradier, *Frivolous Muse*, Salon of 1846, marble, H. 80 ¾ in., Musée des Beaux Arts, Nîmes.

Born to middle-class parents in 1840, Rodin showed an early interest in drawing and enrolled in the École Spéciale de Dessin et de Mathématiques (better known as the Petit École, to distinguish it from the École des Beaux-Arts, which was known as the Grand École), where he was a student from 1854 to 1857. There he spent his mornings copying drawings and antique casts; in the afternoon he went to the Louvre to make copies of paintings and ancient sculptures. In the evenings he attended a drawing class at the Manufacture des Gobelins, where he drew from live models. Rodin soon realized that sculpture was his true calling: "I made separate pieces: arms, heads, feet; next I attacked the entire figure. I understood the grouping immediately... I was in ecstasy."[3] At the conclusion of his studies at the Petit École, he attempted to gain admission to the state-sanctioned École des Beaux-Arts to study sculpture but was rejected each of the three times he applied. Early in his career, he had little success in having his works accepted to the annual Paris Salons. His bitterness at these rejections stayed with him for the rest of his life. Although he continually rebelled against the art establishment and its conservative ideals, he continually sought its recognition and approval.

FIG. 6: Albert-Ernest Carrier-Belleuse, *Bust of a Woman*, circa 1870–1875, terracotta, 24 1/2 × 16 × 11 1/4 in., North Carolina Museum of Art, Raleigh, Purchased with funds from the Lady Marcia Cunliffe-Owen Bequest and the State of North Carolina.

His earliest sculptures, dating from the 1860s, were portrait busts: his father, a priest, a neighborhood workman named Bibi, and his mistress (soon to be the mother of his son) Rose Beuret. However, despite receiving some favorable critical attention, he was unable to support himself as an independent master. Beginning in the late 1860s, he worked for several years in Paris and Brussels under the sculptor Albert-Ernest Carrier-Belleuse, producing decorative groups and busts in plaster and terracotta for the newly emerging bourgeoisie market, patrons who were purchasing works to decorate their homes. Although his status in the studio increased over the years, Rodin eventually fell out with Carrier-Belleuse, who he felt did not fully appreciate him. One of the deciding factors in his decision to leave the studio was that the older master insisted that all of Rodin's creations leave the studio with Carrier's signature on them. *Bust of a Woman* in the NCMA's collection (FIG. 6), which bears Carrier-Belleuse's signature, was probably modeled during the period Rodin spent in the sculptor's studio, and it has been suggested it may have been modeled by Rodin himself. During the first half of the 1870s, Rodin also worked with other artists on several major public sculpture commissions in Brussels and Antwerp.

*"My liberation from academicism was via Michelangelo. He is the bridge by which I crossed from one circle to another."*

AUGUSTE RODIN

In 1875 Rodin exhibited one of his works for the first time at the annual Paris Salon, a marble version of the portrait bust of Bibi, which he titled *Mask of the Man with the Broken Nose* (CAT. 1). Early in the following year, he traveled to Italy to study firsthand the works of Michelangelo and other Renaissance masters. It proved to be a transforming experience for him. He later remarked that Michelangelo's works liberated him from the shackles of academic training and impressed upon him the importance of studying fresh the great sculptors of the past. Rodin returned to Paris with a broader perspective on the history of sculpture but determined to find his own style.

The first independent work Rodin completed after his return from Italy rocked the art establishment—the first of many controversies his works would provoke. The striking realism of the figure—later titled *The Age of Bronze* (FIG. 7)—led to the accusation Rodin had modeled his work from casts taken directly from the human model, a technique considered unworthy of a true sculptor. He was eventually vindicated, and in 1880 the French State purchased a plaster of the work, which was cast in bronze and placed in the Tuileries Gardens. By this time Rodin had been working for more than two years on a second life-size figure, *St. John the Baptist Preaching* (CAT. 3).

During this time Rodin began attracting the attention of other artists. Impressed by his *Mask of the Man with the Broken Nose*, a group of young sculptors at the École des Beaux-Arts went to visit Rodin at his studio. One of them had this to say about the artist: "The first work of Rodin's that I saw was his 'Age of [Bronze],' in the Salon of 1877. Among the real artists it had great success. But the old school, many of whom had made fine things, and were still making them, [disparaged] it to a man. We had thought that it was the most lifelike piece of sculpture that had been produced in French art... and that it was really entitled to the Medal of Honor. We were wild over it. When 'The Broken Nose' was exhibited, we thought that it was the most extraordinary example of modeling, of its kind, that had ever been seen in Paris—worthy of the times of Donatello, and fit to be mentioned with the antique... We left him with the impression that we had seen a great and real artist, a genius, who was sure to be the most powerful demoralizer of what is called 'the sculpture of the École' that we have ever had. At this time, remember, we were all working at the École, and obliged to follow the old manner of study taught there. But Rodin so vividly impressed us that we took a new start, determined to look out for everything that was good, no matter where it came from or who did it. Seeing Rodin gave us new life, in fact it saved us."[4]

The notoriety Rodin gained from *The Age of Bronze* (and very probably his experience working on decorative architectural sculpture commissions in Brussels) helped him secure the commission to create a "decorative portal" for a new Musée des Arts Décoratifs to be built in Paris. Rodin decided to design a set of bas-reliefs representing episodes from the poet Dante Alighieri's journey through hell, described in his early-fourteenth-century epic poem, *The Divine Comedy*. Rodin's *The Gates of Hell* (FIG. 14) constitutes a résumé of the sculptor's interests and preoccupations at the time—Gothic and Renaissance art and architecture (Ghiberti's *Gates of Paradise* for the Baptistery of Florence, in particular), the poetry of Dante and Baudelaire, and, above all, his own powerful response to the beauty and expressive power of the human body.

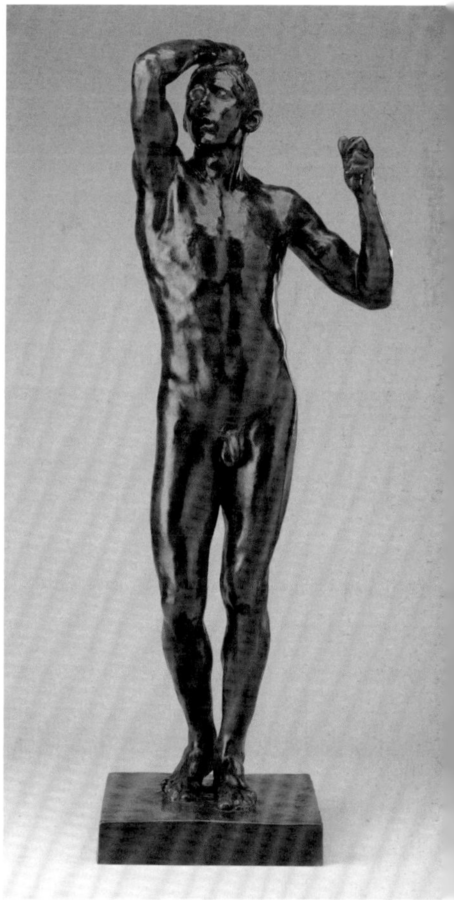

FIG. 7: Auguste Rodin, *The Age of Bronze*, modeled 1876, reduction 1903–1904, cast at a later date, bronze, 41 1/4 × 15 × 13 in., Private collection.

Many of Rodin's single figures and groups from the 1880s onward were originally conceived as players in the human drama of *The Gates*. These progeny—sometimes inverted, fragmented, augmented, and recombined—were often reborn as independent works of art. Rodin later described *The Gates* as his "Noah's Ark." Thirteen of these works are part of the Iris and B. Gerald Cantor Foundation's gift to the NCMA, among them *The Three Shades* (CAT. 4), *Eve* (CAT. 8), *Danaïd* (CAT. 12), *Ugolino and His Sons* (CAT. 6), and Rodin's most celebrated figure, *The Thinker* (CAT. 5). As a commission, however, *The Gates of Hell* was a failure. The Musée des Arts Décoratifs was never built, and *The Gates of Hell*—which Rodin exhibited only once, in 1900, in plaster—was cast in bronze only after the artist's death.

FIG. 8: Iris and B. Gerald Cantor admiring Rodin's *The Gates of Hell*, 1880–1900, Musée Rodin cast 1981, bronze, 250 1/8 × 158 × 33 1/2 in., Iris and B. Gerald Cantor Center for Visual Arts, Stanford University, Gift of the B. Gerald Cantor Collection, 1985.86.

FIG. 9: Auguste Rodin, *The Burghers of Calais*, modeled 1884–1895, Musée Rodin cast 1985, bronze, 82 1/2 × 94 × 95 in., The Metropolitan Museum of Art, New York, Gift of Iris and B. Gerald Cantor, 1989.407.

Between 1878 and 1883, Rodin submitted five unsuccessful proposals for monumental public commissions. In 1884, while he was still intensely involved with *The Gates of Hell*, Rodin was approached by the city of Calais to design a monument commemorating a celebrated episode in its history. A masterpiece in terms of both composition and empathetic rendering of emotion, *The Burghers of Calais* (FIG. 9) represented a turning point in the evolution of the civic monument. It was a rewarding project for Rodin and his first public success.

Unfortunately, more typical was the case with another major public commission by Rodin from the 1890s, his monument to the great novelist Honoré de Balzac. More traditional in its format—a monumental single figure—Rodin's presentation of the writer was arguably his most revolutionary accomplishment. He was offered the commission by the Société des Gens de Lettres, a Parisian literary group, in 1891, and he promised to deliver the statue by January 1893. When the final model was unveiled to the public more than six years after the promised deadline, it was greeted with almost universal derision from critics and the public alike, although many artists rose to his defense. The first bronze cast of this revolutionary statue was not installed in Paris until 1939, twenty-two years after the artist's death. It is now acknowledged as one of the seminal works in the evolution of modern sculpture.

FIG. 10: César, *Portrait of Camille Claudel*, circa 1884, albumen print, Musée Rodin, Paris, Ph. 527. The Metropolitan Museum of Art, New York, Gift of Iris and B. Gerald Cantor, 1989.407.

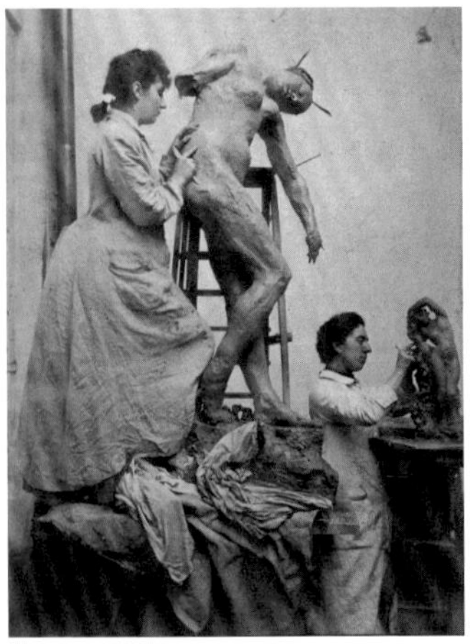

FIG. 11: Camille Claudel in her studio with a model of *Sakountala*, circa 1886–1887. The English sculptor Jesse Lipscomb is at right. Musée Rodin, Ph. 1773.

In 1882 the forty-one-year-old Rodin encountered the seventeen-year-old Camille Claudel (FIGS. 10 and 11) in a sculpture class he was supervising. Impressed by her skill and determination to succeed, Rodin invited her to work in his studio. She soon became more his collaborator—modeling the hands and feet of several of his works—than merely one of the numerous studio assistants he employed. She also became his model, mistress, and muse. Her face and body permeate Rodin's works of the 1880s and 1890s. Several of the figures on *The Gates of Hell* were modeled after her, and the couple's intense (and often difficult) relationship inspired the couples Rodin portrayed during this period: *I Am Beautiful* (CAT. 10), *The Kiss* (CAT. 11), and *Fugitive Love* (CAT. 14). These sculptures, produced during the period when the relationship was at its most rapturous, display an increasing emotional and erotic content and a corresponding sophistication in the poses of the figures. A considerable talent in her own right, Claudel created many extraordinary works, including one Rodin regarded as the finest portrait of himself (CAT. 30). Following the breakup of the relationship in 1898, Claudel's mental state gradually deteriorated. She became obsessed with the idea Rodin had sapped her artistic energies, had fed on her genius. Her psychosis became increasingly acute, and in 1913 her brother Paul had her confined to an asylum, where she remained for the final thirty years of her life.

Rodin's entire approach to sculpture departed radically from long-established academic tradition. He was a pioneer in his conception of the partial figure or fragment as an independent, complete work of art. The first work he sought to publicly exhibit, *Mask of the Man with the Broken Nose* (CAT. 1), modeled 1863–64, was a partial figure. The cold temperature in Rodin's studio caused the back portion of the head to detach and fall off. Instead of restoring the work to its original state, Rodin decided to leave it as it was, in its fragmentary state. He later declared the piece "**determined all my future work ... I have kept that mask before my mind in everything I have done.**"[5] Perhaps inspired by the fragments of ancient sculpture he had studied in the Louvre and on his trip to Italy in 1876, Rodin continued to experiment with partial figures during the 1870s. By the 1890s he was clearly thinking of these fragmentary figures as complete, independent works of art, and he began exhibiting and selling them as such. Many of these works had their origins in preliminary studies for monuments such as *The Gates of Hell*, *The Burghers of Calais*, and *Balzac*. One of Rodin's assistants described his studio as crowded with "fragments of sculptures in work, casts of all sorts, heads, torsos, arms and legs ... He had several plaster casts [of his works] made. One was kept intact, the others were cut apart, and the sections numbered and catalogued, so they might be taken out of their cupboards to serve in other figures, perhaps years later. Thus dissected, limb from torso, they would be set, again and again, in new arrangements and further groupings."[6] Many of Rodin's works, such as *I Am Beautiful* (CAT. 10) and *Toilette of Venus and Andromeda* (CAT. 13), were created from two originally distinct figures.

FIG. 12: Auguste Rodin, *The Prayer*, modeled 1910, Musée Rodin cast 1979, bronze, 49 1/2 × 21 5/8 × 19 5/8 in., North Carolina Museum of Art, Raleigh, Gift of the Iris and B. Gerald Cantor Foundation.

He regularly omitted hands, feet, arms, and even heads from his figures, paring away what he considered extraneous in order to express the essence of his subject. Rodin applied the same surgical rigor, whether producing a portrait or figure, giving form to a historical or literary theme, or even to an abstract concept such as motion, as he sought the most dramatic and concise forms to convey ideas with maximum impact (FIG. 12). Within the still-dominant academic tradition, these fragments were criticized as mutilated, ugly, and even morbid and sadistic violations of established standards. Today, however, Rodin's explorations of the "partial" figure are considered to represent a crossroads in the evolution of sculpture, and they are perhaps his most significant legacy to modern sculpture.

During the late 1880s and 1890s, Rodin's artistic career was sharply on the rise. A number of the "progeny" from *The Gates of Hell* appeared in numerous exhibitions, generating a great deal of interest in artistic circles, first in Europe, and then in America. Critics, artists, politicians, and patrons flocked to his studio. In 1889 his works were paired with the paintings of his contemporary Claude Monet, another titan of the artistic avant-garde, in a major exhibition at the prestigious Galerie Georges Petit. The exhibition attracted huge crowds of visitors and received considerable critical attention, marking a turning point in the public appreciation of both artists. Rodin's sculptures were exhibited in Switzerland, Belgium, and the Netherlands. He organized a personal retrospective exhibition that included 168 of his works in plaster, bronze, and marble, displayed in a special pavilion adjacent to the 1900 Universal Exposition in Paris, which brought him to the attention of an even larger international public. In the introduction to the catalogue of the exhibition, Monet predicted the exhibition would be "the definitive consecration of a beautiful artist," and it was.[7] Orders for his works and requests for exhibitions poured in from around the globe: Great Britain, Denmark, Germany, the United States, Canada, Japan, and Argentina. By the end of the first decade of the twentieth century, Rodin was the most famous sculptor—if not artist—in the world. His studio at the Villa des Brilliants in Meudon, on the outskirts of Paris (which he purchased in 1895), became a destination for kings, politicians, aristocrats, critics—and the general public. By this time he had become an artist-entrepreneur, employing some fifty assistants to meet the demand for his plasters, bronzes, and marbles, which could be produced in different sizes according to a patron's wishes.

In 1905 Rodin began renting rooms in the Hôtel Biron in Paris, where he would live and work until his death on November 17, 1917. He was buried at Meudon on November 24 amid great pomp, his funeral attended by dignitaries from several countries. A monumental-size cast of *The Thinker* sits above his grave there (FIG. 13). In the years before his death, Rodin entered into lengthy negotiations with the French government, offering to donate his entire oeuvre, on the condition the Hôtel Biron, which was owned by the French government, would be converted into a museum for his work and collection. In accordance with Rodin's will, the Musée Rodin was given the right to cast Rodin's sculptures posthumously to pay for the costs of its operation. A 1956 French law limited production to twelve casts of each model. A system of numbering was established by French legislation in 1968 whereby the first eight casts were to be made available to the public for purchase and the last four reserved for public institutions. Nearly all of the sculptures in the Cantor Foundation gift were cast by authority of this legislation, under the supervision of the Musée Rodin.

FIG. 13: Pierre Choumoff, *Rodin's Funeral at Meudon*, November 24, 1917, gelatin-silver print, Musée Rodin, Paris, Ph. 1009.

1 Charles Baudelaire, Le Salon de 1846, XVI, "Pourquoi la sculpture est ennuyeuse," XVIII, "De L'Héroïsme de la vie moderne," in Kelley 1975, pp. 177, 180.

2 Paul Mantz, "L'École des beaux-arts: Les concours, les envois de Rome," *Gazette des beaux-arts*, 1869, IV, pp. 121–23, in Fusco and Janson 1980, p. 14.

3 Dujardin-Beaumetz 1913, in Elsen 1965, pp. 145–46.

4 Bartlett 1889, in Elsen 1965, pp. 41–42.

5 Bartlett 1889, in Elsen 1965, p. 21.

6 Frisch and Shipley 1939, pp. 186, 113.

7 Butler 1980, p. 101.

Q Théophile Thoré, quoted in Thoré 1868, p. 558.

Q August Rodin, in a letter to his former pupil the sculptor Antoine Bourdelle, quoted in Varnedoe 1985, p. 19.

# *Catalogue*

## 1 MASK OF THE MAN WITH THE BROKEN NOSE

Modeled 1863–1864, Musée Rodin cast 1978
Bronze
12 1/2 × 7 1/4 × 6 in. (31.8 x 18.4 × 15.2 cm)
Gift of the Iris and B. Gerald Cantor Foundation, 2009 (2009.1.1)

One of Rodin's earliest surviving works, *Mask of the Man with the Broken Nose*, was a portrait of a workman named Bibi, who lived in the Parisian neighborhood where Rodin had moved in 1863. Rodin's original clay model was probably made late the same year. During the following harsh winter, the clay model froze and cracked in his unheated studio, and the back portion of the head broke off. Rather than repair or abandon the work, Rodin instinctively realized the expressive power of the damaged head and submitted a plaster version of the sculpture to the Paris Salon of 1865. This innovative approach and the brutal ugliness of the man's features (particularly his battered nose) were at odds with contemporary canons of taste and ideal beauty, and the unidealized work was refused by the Salon jury. Rodin made other models of the head and restored one of them to its original form, completing the head and reworking the hair, to which he added a fillet. He exhibited a plaster version of the restored bust in 1872 and commissioned his longtime friend (and later assistant) Léon Fourquet to carve a marble version, which he then submitted to the Salon of 1875 (FIG. 1A). The marble was accepted, marking the first time one of Rodin's works was admitted into the Salon. It was subsequently cast in bronze in at least two different sizes. A smaller variant of the head appears twice on the tympanum of *The Gates of Hell*.

Rodin also took another model of the head (perhaps the original damaged one), completely hollowed out the back, and trimmed the edges to create the "mask," which he cast in bronze and exhibited at the Salon of 1878. Critics noted its battered features resembled those of Michelangelo, whose nose had been broken in a fight with a fellow student, as portrayed in the well-known portrait bust by the Renaissance sculptor Daniele da Volterra, exhibited the same year at the Exposition Universelle in Paris (FIG. 1B).

Rodin's initial inspiration for *Mask of the Man with the Broken Nose* may have been one of the classical heads the artist studied in the Louvre or in Italy (perhaps one similar to the *Bust of Homer*, FIG. 1C), and this may in turn have influenced his decision to have it carved in marble. His friend and biographer Judith Cladel noted, "Rodin made a bust of a man and strove to portray the energy and imposing simplicity that had astonished him in the ancient busts and the statue of *The Knife Grinder* that he had seen in the galleries of the Louvre."[1] One of Rodin's earliest biographers noted, after conversations with the artist, that "the man's face resembled types common in ancient Greece and Rome."[2] A version of the bust was "discovered" in a secondhand dealer's shop by a friend of Rodin's, the artist Jules Desbois, who brought it to the École des Beaux-Arts for examination by the École's professors. They praised it as an antique head of high quality. After hearing them express their admiration, Desbois "unmasked" it as a work by Rodin, who, he noted, "failed three times to gain entrance into the École, and this piece, which you all thought was an antique, was rejected by the Salon."[3]

FIG. 1A: Auguste Rodin, *Man with a Broken Nose*, 1875, marble, 17 1/2 × 16 1/4 × 9 1/2 in., Musée Rodin, Paris, S. 974.

FIG. 1B: Daniele da Volterra, *Portrait Bust of Michelangelo*, 1564–1566, bronze, H. 11 4/5 in., Musée du Louvre, Paris, inventory no. RF2385.

FIG. 1C: Roman, *Bust of Homer*, 2nd century C.E., after a 2nd-century B.C.E. Greek original, marble, H. 20 3/4 in., Musée du Louvre, Paris, inventory no. Ma440.

*"Rodin's motive in modeling this head, the head of an aging, ugly man, whose broken nose even helped to emphasize the tortured expression of his face, must have been the fullness of life that was cumulated in these features... This face had not been touched by life; it had been permeated through and through with it as though an inexorable hand had thrust it into fate and held it there as in the whirlpool of a washing, gnawing torrent."*

RAINER MARIA RILKE

Thus, at the very outset of his career as a sculptor, Rodin had the good fortune, thanks to an accident, to create a work that would have profound repercussions for the rest of his life, one that would influence his whole approach to his art. As one recent Rodin scholar wrote, "The *Mask* was Rodin's talisman because it taught him how to capitalize on chance and accident. When the frozen portion of the head fell off, Rodin was confronted with the question that haunted him for much of his later life and led to his partial figures. What could sculpture do without? What was essential?"[4] Near the end of his life, Rodin acknowledged the seminal importance of this work: "That mask determined all of my future work. It was the first good piece of modeling I ever did... I have kept that mask before my mind in everything I have done... In fact, I have never succeeded in making a figure as good as 'The Broken Nose.'"[5]

1 Cladel 1917, pp. 53–54.

2 Lawton 1906, p. 25.

3 Cladel 1936, p. 91.

4 Elsen 2003, p. 441. Elsen's entries on Rodin's *Mask* and *Head of the Man with the Broken Nose* (pp. 438–44) are exemplary.

5 Bartlett 1889, in Elsen 1965, p. 21.

Q Elsen 1965, p. 119.

"That mask determined all of my future work. It was the first good piece of modeling I ever did…I have kept that mask before my mind in everything I have done…In fact, I have never succeeded in making a figure as good as 'The Broken Nose.'"

## 2 THE CALL TO ARMS (LA DÉFENSE)

Modeled 1879, cast at a later date
Bronze
44 1/2 × 22 1/2 × 15 in. (113 × 57.2 × 38.4 cm)
Gift of the Iris and B. Gerald Cantor Foundation, 2009 (2009.1.2)

Throughout the nineteenth century, French municipalities generated numerous competitions for sculpture commissions both to honor great men and historic events and to inspire national and civic pride. Winning one of these competitions was one of the best ways for a young artist to establish his reputation.

Rodin submitted this dramatic group as his entry for a monument to be composed of two figures commemorating the courage of Parisians in defending their city during the Franco-Prussian War in 1870. He represented a female figure personifying the Spirit of Liberty hurling herself against the enemy with outstretched arms, clenched fists, and a scream of defiance. The starting point for the sculpture was François Rude's *The Spirit of Liberty* (*La Marseillaise*) on the Arc de Triomphe in Paris (FIG. 2A), which Rodin called a "sublime poem to war."[1] Both Rude's and Rodin's figures wear a Phrygian cap, a symbol of the Republic, and both figures fly forward, exhorting their supporters with gesture and voice. However, there are marked differences between Rude's more noble and dignified group and Rodin's raw and dramatic presentation of the subject. Rather than a call of exhortation and encouragement to those behind her, Rodin's Liberty shrieks a defiant war cry. Rather than garbed in armor and holding a sword, she is represented nude above the waist, her lower body enveloped in a molten mass of drapery, her hands balled into fists as she hurls herself outward against the enemy. The outstretched arms and the upward and outward surge of Rodin's Liberty recall Carpeaux's sculptural group *La Danse* on the facade of the Paris Opéra, a work Rodin admired, or even some of the dynamic sculptures he produced in Carrier-Belleuse's studio during the period he was working there (FIG. 2B). Collapsing against her is the nude figure of a warrior grasping a broken sword, which supports his weakened body. He looks up to Liberty to find comfort or perhaps some acknowledgment of his sacrifice, but she ignores him as she surges forward in her frenzy. One of Liberty's wings is bent back, complementing the bent leg of the wounded soldier, whose pose recalls both Michelangelo's *Pietà* in the Cathedral of Florence and his unfinished *St. Matthew* in the Accademia in Florence (FIG. 2C). The bent wing may have been inspired by the one on Rude's Liberty, where it is so represented by necessity, since it is shown in relief, but in Rodin's work it may suggest that she (personifying French liberty), like the soldier, is also vulnerable.

Rodin's entry was eliminated in the first round of the competition by the selection committee, who ultimately awarded the commission to Louis-Ernest Barrias's more traditional submission. The spiraling rhythms and agitated profiles of the work lacked the decorum required of public statuary of the day. Rodin's collapsing warrior must have seemed insufficiently heroic, a charge later leveled against his subsequent submission for a public monument *The Burghers of Calais*, and his figure of Liberty grotesque and ignoble. "There were at least sixty sculptors competing," Rodin later said, "but in spite of all my efforts, in spite of the life which I believe animates my group *The Call to Arms*, I was not even considered ... Truly, I could not compete against Barrias and [Antonin] Mercié. My group must have appeared too violent, too impassioned. So little progress has been made since Rude's *Marseillaise*, which also screams with all its strength."[2]

Despite his disappointment, Rodin continued to exhibit the sculpture, and it gradually began to attract favorable attention from critics. In the catalogue of Rodin's 1900 retrospective exhibition, the critic Arsène Alexandre described the group: "A robust combatant, fatally wounded, staggers and falls, while a sort of ferocious Valkyrie, the Spirit of War, howling, grimacing with rage, flings out her arms in exasperation, intoxicated by the carnage and, face against the wind, sings her hymn to death."[3] Thirty-seven years after creating his initial model, Rodin successfully proposed *The Call to Arms* for a commission to honor the heroic sacrifice of the French defenders of Verdun during the First World War. On August 1, 1920, nearly three years after the artist's death, a fifteen-foot bronze version of Rodin's sculpture was erected near the entrance to Verdun.

1 Gsell 1911, ed. 1984, p. 36.

2 Coquiot 1917, p. 107.

3 Alexandre 1900, CAT. 70.

FIG. 2A: François Rude, *The Spirit of Liberty (La Marseillaise)*, 1833–1836, stone, approx. 504 × 336 in., Arc de Triomphe, Paris.

FIG. 2B: Albert-Ernest Carrier-Belleuse, perhaps with the assistance of Auguste Rodin, *The Abduction of Hippodamia*, modeled circa 1877, cast at a later date, bronze, 30 × 23 × 12 in., Collection of Lynne and Mark Hammerschlag.

FIG. 2C: Michelangelo Buonarotti, *St. Matthew*, circa 1506, marble, H. 106 5/8 in., Galleria dell'Accademia, Florence, inventory no. 1077.

## 3 ST. JOHN THE BAPTIST PREACHING (REDUCTION)

Modeled circa 1880, Musée Rodin cast 1974
Bronze
19 3/4 × 11 × 9 1/8 in. (50.2 × 27.9 × 23.2 cm)
Gift of the Iris and B. Gerald Cantor Foundation, 2009 (2009.1.3)

Rodin said this figure was inspired by a peasant from the Abruzzi region of Italy who came to his studio seeking work as a model: "Seeing him, I was seized with admiration; that rough hairy man, expressing in his bearing and physical strength all the violence, but also all the mystical character of his race. I thought immediately of a John the Baptist; that is, a man of nature, a visionary, a believer, a forerunner who came to announce one greater than himself. The peasant undressed, mounted the model stand as if he had never posed; he planted himself, head up, torso straight, at the same time supported on his two legs, opened like a compass. The movement was so right, so determined, and so true that I cried: 'But it's a walking man!' I immediately resolved to make what I had seen…I only copied the model whom chance had sent me."[1]

The rough, sinewy physique and angular features of Rodin's *St. John* were very different from other late-eighteenth- and nineteenth-century representations of the saint. These expressive qualities find their closest parallels in contemporary literary descriptions of biblical personages as ordinary individuals and the Baptist as a rough and violent preacher.[2]

Traditionally wearing a garment of camel's hair and holding a reed cross, John the Baptist was typically represented in the act of blessing, gesturing toward, or baptizing Christ. Rodin rejected these conventions. His Baptist is God's messenger, a determined, itinerant preacher, "the voice of one crying in the wilderness, 'Prepare ye the way of the Lord.'"[3] Like *The Age of Bronze*, Rodin's earliest life-size statue, the figure of John is nude. While this may have been acceptable for a mythological or generic subject like *The Age of Bronze*, to contemporary viewers it must have exceeded traditional boundaries of proper decorum for representing a biblical personage. At one point Rodin considered adding the traditional attribute of the reed cross, perhaps to clarify the identity of the figure, but he soon decided against it. By stripping away all of the Baptist's traditional attributes—including his hair shirt—Rodin made the body and pose of the figure the sole iconographic "keys" to his identity. The emphatic musculature of the figure, particularly evident in the back and arms, underscores the intensity of the Baptist's message. At the same time his leanness, hollow eyes, and sunken cheeks remind the viewer he lived the ascetic existence of a desert hermit.

Like many of the works Rodin would create early in his career, *St. John* bears the unmistakable influence of Italian Renaissance sculpture (in particular the works of Donatello). The tensely muscled torso turns to the left, following the pull of the head, while the outward-thrusting right arm, which traditionally pointed to the object of the Baptist's words "Behold the Lamb of God" (John 1:29), extends into our space, as if to suggest the prophesied Messiah is here among us. The muscles of his rear leg have begun to tense as they prepare to propel the figure forward, while the outstretched front leg is solidly planted, the knee locked. The position of the legs was seen by critics as ambiguous: was the figure standing still or moving forward? This issue was addressed in a conversation in 1911 on "movement in art" between Rodin and the French writer Paul Gsell. Gsell begins, "One feels a mysterious and formidable power stirs and pushes [the figure]. So walking, usually such a banal movement, here becomes grandiose because it is the fulfillment of a divine mission." Rodin picks up the conversation, stating that if he had depicted the Baptist using a pose taken from a high-speed photograph of a model walking, even though the figure would have been caught in "full action," he would have seemed "suddenly frozen in mid-air."

**What Rodin sought to represent in *St. John* was, in his own words, "the gradual unfolding of movement."[4]**

Rodin exhibited a larger-than-life plaster of *St. John* at the Salon of 1880 and a bronze version the following year, arousing both criticism and praise for its directness and realism. The bronze was purchased for the Musée du Luxembourg (the state museum of contemporary art) in 1884, but it was relegated to the darkest corner of the museum.

FIG. 3A: Auguste Rodin, *Torso of a Man (Study for St. John the Baptist Preaching)*, 1878, Musée Rodin cast 1979, bronze, 21 × 10 3/4 × 15 in., Iris and B. Gerald Cantor Center for Visual Arts, Stanford University, Gift of the B. Gerald Cantor Collection, 1983.200.

Rodin's one-time pupil Antoine Bourdelle used *St. John* to compare Rodin to an earlier master whose works were likewise both praised and condemned for their directness: **"In this old Saint John, one could almost say that the Amsterdam master, the elderly Rembrandt, has laid aside his glorious brushes, and with his magnificent hands has kneaded this entire, demented, frenzied statue, whose profiles are bitten like one of his thick, black etchings."[5]** Other young artists were also deeply impressed. One of them declared, "He goes deeper into a subject than any living artist. Look at his 'St. John' in the Luxembourg. He has finished that subject; it is the great note of this century. We have never had a sculptor who could interpret nature as he does."[6] The critics and public eventually came to appreciate Rodin's *St. John*. In addition to the Luxembourg cast, two full-size bronzes and at least twenty versions in three different sizes were issued between 1899 and 1908. The head of the Baptist was also cast separately as an independent work about 1883.

1 Dujardin-Beaumetz 1913, in Elsen 1965, p. 166.

2 See De Caso and Sanders 1973, pp. 75, 79, nn. 15–16.

3 Mark 1:3 (KJV). Rodin was also probably inspired by John the Baptist's own words (Luke 3:4–17).

4 Gsell 1911, pp. 56–59. Rodin continued, "It is the artist who tells the truth and photography that lies."

5 "Rodin et la sculpture," *Revue des études franco-russes* (September 1909), p. 376, in Le Normand-Romain 2007, II, p. 644.

6 Bartlett 1889, in Elsen 1965, p. 42.

"He goes deeper into a subject than any living artist. Look at his 'St. John' in the Luxembourg. He has finished that subject; it is the great note of this century. We have never had a sculptor who could interpret nature as he does."

## *THE GATES OF HELL* AND ITS OFFSPRING

Impressed by Rodin's *The Age of Bronze* (FIG. 7) and *St. John the Baptist* (CAT. 3), Edmond Turquet, the French undersecretary of fine arts, considered Rodin "a great artist, one capable of executing any task confided to him," and personally arranged the artist's first important public commission in Paris.[1] In August 1880 the French minister of public instruction charged Rodin with executing, for the sum of eight thousand francs, the model of a sculpted door for the Museum of Decorative Arts, depicting in bas-relief scenes from Dante's *The Divine Comedy*.[2] Since there was no official competition for the commission, the decision to use Dante's text as the literary inspiration was probably Rodin's. His friend and earliest biographer, Judith Cladel, wrote that Rodin was obsessed by Dante's text, which he constantly carried in his pocket and "read and reread ... and made a sort of commentary in the form of innumerable sketches." The eternal character and "internal drama" of the poem "seduced and subjugated the sculptor ... The monument that he was going to erect would be of an internal drama, the revolt of man against the supreme power—which in his youth had often obsessed his religious spirit. This would be *The Gates of Hell*."[3]

As Rodin continued to labor on the project over the next twenty years, however, his conception of the theme evolved further and further from the narrative structure of *The Divine Comedy*. Themes from Baudelaire's *The Flowers of Evil*, which Rodin was illustrating during this period; from the Bible; and from classical mythology became mixed with those from Dante's poem, so that *The Gates* became a cauldron of human activity (in the words of a contemporary writer, **"the gathering, in eventful motion, of the instincts, the fatalities, the desires, the despairs of everything that cries out and groans in man"**) drawn from many sources, including the artist's personal experiences as well as his fertile imagination.[4] Only three of the main figural groups that remained on *The Gates* at the time of Rodin's death actually derived directly from Dante (CATS. 4, 6, and 11). *The Gates of Hell* was not only a sculptural project but also an architectural one. As Dante's work was the literary starting point, the initial architectural models for *The Gates* were compartmentalized portals made for medieval and Renaissance churches, chief among them Ghiberti's bronze doors, made between 1425 and 1450 for the Baptistery in Florence, which Michelangelo had named *Gates of Paradise*. Rodin's initial intent was to follow the general format of Ghiberti's doors, creating a series of narrative bas-reliefs framed within an architectural armature. However, just as his conception of the theme evolved further and further from the narrative of *The Divine Comedy*, Rodin eventually relinquished the idea of Ghiberti's formal composition. The more he worked, the further he abandoned the gridlike structure of the traditional doors and the clarity of individual bas-reliefs, modeling instead a floating and churning tide of human figures, many modeled almost completely in the round. Works by other artists—the *Last Judgments* of medieval and Renaissance sculptors like Nicola Pisano and Lorenzo Maitani, Michelangelo's Sistine Chapel fresco, and paintings by earlier nineteenth-century artists like Géricault (*Raft of the Medusa*) and Delacroix (*Barque of Dante*)—also helped mold Rodin's conception of the project.

Some of the closest visual and iconographic parallels for *The Gates* are found in representations (both sculptural and painted) of the Last Judgment. The poet Rainer Maria Rilke, who briefly (from 1905 to 1906) served as Rodin's personal secretary, strikes an apocalyptic tone in his description of *The Gates*: "He has endowed hundreds and hundreds of figures that were barely larger than his hand with the life of every passion, the flowering of every pleasure, and the burden of every vice. He has created bodies that touched each other all over, clung

FIG. 14: Auguste Rodin, *The Gates of Hell*, 1880–1900, Musée Rodin cast 1981, bronze, 250 5/8 × 157 9/10 × 33 1/2 in., Iris and B. Gerald Cantor Center for Visual Arts, Stanford University, Gift of the B. Gerald Cantor Collection, 1985.86.

The Three Shades
The Thinker
Toilette of Venus and Andromeda
Fallen Caryatid
I Am Beautiful
The Prayer
The Falling Man
Ugolino
Fugitive Love (Fugit Amor)
Fugitive Love (Fugit Amor)

together like animals that have sunk their teeth into each other, and fell like a single living organism into the abyss; bodies that listen like faces, that take flight like arms raised to hurl something, chains of bodies, like garlands and vine tendrils; and heavy clusters of human forms into which the sap of sin rises from the roots of pain."[5]

The French poet, journalist, and novelist Anatole France observed a very insightful distinction between Rodin's *The Gates of Hell* and earlier *Last Judgments*: "In these [earlier] representations of theological hell, sinners are tormented by horned devils...In Rodin's hell there are no more devils, or at least the devils are hidden within the damned. The evil spirits who make these men and women suffer are their passions, their loves, and their hatreds, their flesh and their thoughts...It is to discover with sympathy that Rodin's hell is no longer one of vengeance; it is a hell of tenderness and pity."[6]

Many of Rodin's single figures and groups from the 1880s onward were originally conceived as players in the human drama of *The Gates* (left), which Rodin called his "Noah's Ark." These progeny—sometimes inverted, fragmented, or recombined—were reborn as independent works of art and exhibited as such. As a commission, however, *The Gates of Hell* was a failure. It cost the French government far more than eight thousand francs agreed upon in the original contract. The Museum of Decorative Arts was never built, and *The Gates* was cast in bronze only after the artist's death.

1 Elsen 1960 remains the most thorough and readable source on the commission. Turquet's remarks were quoted by Bartlett 1889, in Elsen 1965, p. 66.

2 The actual decree is reproduced in Elsen 1960, p. 4 (FIG. 1); also see p. 249, n. 1.

3 "La Jeunesse de Rodin," *Revue universelle* (May 1, 1935), p. 320; ibid., 1950, p. 139.

4 Gustave Geffroy, in Monet-Rodin 1889/1989, p. 57.

5 Elsen 1965, pp. 127–28.

6 "La Porte de l'Enfer," *Le Figaro*, June 7, 1900; reprinted in Butler 1980, p. 106 (trans. John Anzalone).

## 4 THE THREE SHADES

Modeled circa 1886, enlarged circa 1901, Musée Rodin cast 1981
Bronze
75 1/2 × 75 1/2 × 42 in. (191.8 × 191.8 × 106.7 cm)
Gift of the Iris and B. Gerald Cantor Foundation, 2009 (2009.1.5)

FIG. 4A: Auguste Rodin, *Adam*, modeled 1877–1879, Musée Rodin cast 1974, bronze, 76 1/4 × 29 1/2 × 30 1/2 in., Iris and B. Gerald Cantor Center for Visual Arts, Stanford University, Gift of Iris and B. Gerald Cantor, 1985.15.

In Canto XVI of the *Inferno* (5–87), Dante meets three shades, souls of his Florentine countrymen, who move continuously in a circle as they tell of their woeful state in Hades. The three shades were one of the few subjects drawn directly from Dante's poem to remain part of *The Gates*, as Rodin labored on the project over more than twenty years. From the beginning *The Three Shades* stood upon the top lintel of *The Gates of Hell*, crowning the tympanum just above *The Thinker*. They were derived from Rodin's *Adam* (FIG. 4A), which he intended to flank *The Gates*, together with a pendant figure of *Eve* (CAT. 8, FIG. 4B), but since the two figures were not part of the original plan, his request to include them was denied.[1]

The most remarkable aspect of the work is that the three figures—even their pedestals—are identical, seen from the left, straight on, and from the right. The three figures radiate from a single point where their left arms converge, like spokes on a wheel, following Dante's description: "They all three made of themselves a wheel" ("Fenno una rota di se tutti e trei," *Inferno*, Canto XVI, 20). In this enlarged version, the repetition of the figures—and the spatial intervals between them—becomes much more emphatic. The repetitive, relentless aspect of the figures emphasizes their tragic character. As one Rodin scholar wrote, "Seemingly drawn together and down by the force of gravity, they embody a feeling of helplessness which is depersonalized by being presented in triplicate. It is like the representation of a line in a poem which gains in force, each time it is repeated. In grouping three casts of this self-engrossed figure, Rodin ruled out any possibility of communication between them. Their physical closeness is deceptive. No consolation is possible."[2]

Rodin's use of multiple *identical* figures in a single ensemble was unprecedented. Both Dante and he would have recognized the parallels among these three figures and ancient mythological trios, in particular the three Fates, who determined the span of one's earthly existence. Certainly Rodin would have been familiar with neoclassical and nineteenth-century sculpture groups that featured three figures, like Canova's *Three Graces*, or the three dancers who circle around the base of Jean-Baptiste Carpeaux's *La Danse* on the facade of the Opéra in Paris.[3] In these two works, the presentation of three figures in a roughly circular arrangement offered the viewer the experience of simultaneously seeing a similar nude figure from three different angles. Rodin's use of a single figure, repeated three times, represents a distinctly different conception. There is nothing of the clever variation or the decorative, rhythmic vitality that informs the earlier groups, and there is no variation in

> *"Dante is more profound and has more fire than I have been able to represent. He is a literary sculptor. He speaks in gestures as well as in words, is precise and comprehensive not only in sentiment and idea, but in the movement of the body."*
>
> AUGUSTE RODIN

the figures. The identical, massive heads and bodies of his shades—Dante described them as "wrestlers"—are arranged at the same level. They are unyielding, relentless in their monotony.

Rodin's use of identical figures may have its origins in Dante's text. Canto III of the *Inferno* opens with the words Dante and Virgil read inscribed on the summit of the gateway leading to hell:

*Per me si va nella città dolente,*
Through me is the way into the doleful city
*per me si va ne l'etterno dolore,*
Through me is the way into eternal suffering
*per me si va tra la perduta gente.*
Through me is the way that runs among the lost.

Here Dante employed a literary device known as anaphora—a deliberate repetition of a phrase at the beginning of a stanza used for emphasis or dramatic effect. Rodin's shades can be understood as a visual anaphora inspired by Dante's lines. In the original plan of *The Gates*, the Shades pointed downward to the very portals to which Dante's lines referred. The stanza inscribed on Dante's infernal gateway concluded with the words *Lasciate ogni speranza, voi ch'entrate* (Abandon all hope, ye who enter here). [4]

FIG. 4B: *Adam* and *Eve* flanking Auguste Rodin's *The Gates of Hell*, 1880–1900, Musée Rodin cast 1981, bronze, 250 5/8 × 157 9/10 × 33 1/2 in., Iris and B. Gerald Cantor Center for Visual Arts, Stanford University, Gift of the B. Gerald Cantor Collection, 1985.86.

1 Cladel 1936, p. 140.

2 Tancock 1967, p. 39.

3 Bernard Barryte, curator of European Art at the Iris and B. Gerald Cantor Center for Visual Arts, Stanford University, suggested (*in litteris*) to the author that another influence on Rodin may have been the two fishermen in Raphael's cartoon for his tapestry *The Miraculous Draught of Fishes* (Victoria and Albert Museum), which the sculptor may have seen on one of his visits to London (the first in 1881) or known through a reproduction.

4 The entire stanza is as follows: "Per me si va nella città dolente, / per me si va nell'eterno dolore, / per me si va tra la perduta gente. / Giustizia mosse il mio alto fattore; / fecemi la divina podestate, / la somma sapïenza e 'l primo amore. / Dinanzi a me non fuor cose create / se non etterne, e io etterno duro. Lasciate ogne speranza, voi ch'intrate" (Dante 1975, *Inferno*, III, 1–9).

Q Bartlett 1889, in Elsen 1965, p. 69.

## 5 THE THINKER

Modeled 1880, reduced in 1903, this example cast at a later date
Bronze
14 3/4 × 7 7/8 × 11 3/8 in. (37.5 × 20 × 28.9 cm)
Gift of the Iris and B. Gerald Cantor Foundation, in honor of Governor Michael F. Easley and Mary P. Easley, 2009 (2009.1.6)

*The Thinker* sits high in the center of *The Gates of Hell* and was probably the first sculpture Rodin created for it. Since the initial inspiration for *The Gates* was Dante's *Inferno*, Dante himself was the initial inspiration for Rodin's surmounting figure. Rodin—who clearly identified with the figure—had this to say about how *The Thinker* came into being, and what he symbolizes: "In the days long gone by, I conceived of the idea of *The Gates of Hell*. Before the door, seated on a rock, Dante, thinking of the plan of his poem. Behind him Ugolino, Francesca, Paolo, all the characters of the Divine Comedy. This project was not realized. Thin, ascetic, Dante in his straight robe separated from the whole would have been without meaning. Guided by my first inspiration, I conceived another thinker, a naked man, seated upon a rock, his feet drawn under him, his fist against his teeth, he dreams. The fertile thought slowly elaborates itself within his brain. He is no longer dreamer, he is creator."[1] Rodin first exhibited the work under the title *The Poet* in 1888, but by the following year, he had added *The Thinker* to the title (*The Thinker, The Poet: Fragment from The Gates*).

*The Thinker* has a number of illustrious sculptural progenitors. Among them are Michelangelo's marble figure of Lorenzo de' Medici (known as "Il Pensiero," "the pensive one," or "the Thinker"), who sits in contemplation above his cenotaph in the Medici Chapel in Florence (FIG. 5A), which Rodin sketched in Italy in 1876, and the tormented figure of Ugolino in Jean-Baptiste Carpeaux's *Ugolino and His Sons* (FIG. 6A), exhibited at the Paris Salon of 1863.[2] Rodin moved beyond these starting points, however. *The Thinker*'s muscles are more pronounced. He leans forward, compressing his mass. Bringing the right arm across the body while moving the thighs and left arm in a counter-direction, Rodin enhanced the torsion of the figure, endowing it with an inner tension, a restless energy at odds with its seated pose.[3] Lips compressed together in a grimace by the knuckles of his right hand, his expression intense, Rodin's *The Thinker* is imbued with a brooding melancholy absent from Michelangelo's more cerebral figure. The critic Arsène Alexandre attributed the differences between the *Thinkers* of Michelangelo and Rodin to the times in which they were created: "Our epoch is forced to say much more to express as much. We are no longer in the time when one could be strong without effort. Today, thought is devoted to bitterness, to distresses, to the crushing. The most rough and austere conceptions of Michelangelo are calm and serene compared to those we have at present. The heroes and thinkers of the great Florentine are saddened by the memory of light. This thinker of Rodin seems to have known only shadow."[4] As Rodin himself stated, "What makes my *Thinker* think is that he thinks not only with his brain, with his knitted brow, his distended nostrils and compressed lips, but with every muscle of his arms, back and legs, with his clenched fist and gripping toes."[5]

An enlarged version of *The Thinker* was installed in front of the Panthéon in Paris in 1904, Rodin's first work to be placed in a prominent outdoor location in the French capital. A number of factors—its pose, its emphatic profiles, the absence of any attributes linking it to a specific subject or time (thereby connecting it to all eras)—led to its eventual status as a cultural icon (as early as 1908 it was used in an advertisement), and by midcentury *The Thinker* had become the most familiar work of sculpture ever created. That it *is* so familiar actually prevents the viewer from seeing it as a work of art; rather, it has become a visual cliché, the subject of caricatures, cartoons, advertisements, and trinkets. But *The Thinker* never lost its significance for Rodin, who clearly identified with the figure. Rodin scholar Albert Elsen described *The Thinker* as "a projection of Rodin the sculptor, and the artist in general, who confronts his own times and is judge of them."[6] Rodin remained bound to the figure even in death. He requested it be placed over his grave at Meudon. There, inscribed on the pedestal between the figure and Rodin's remains, is a single word: RODIN (FIG. 5B).

1 Letter to the critic Marcel Adam, reprinted in *Gil Blas* (Paris, July 7, 1904), in Elsen 1985b, p. 43.

2 Rodin may also have been inspired by the unhappy figure being pulled downward into hell in the lower right quadrant of Michelangelo's Sistine Chapel *Last Judgment* fresco.

3 Roger Fry wrote that "even the stillness of his Penseur is only the equilibrium of opposed forces each at the utmost limit of intensity" ("The Sculptures of Maillol," *Burlington Magazine*, XVII [April 1910], p. 27).

4 Arsène Alexandre, "Auguste Rodin—Le Penseur," *Chroniques d'art* (Paris, May 1909), in Elsen 1985b, p. 89.

5 Marcel Adam, op. cit., in Elsen 1963, p. 52.

6 Elsen 1960, p. 129. Elsewhere Elsen (1985b, p. 71) described *The Thinker* as "a spiritual portrait of Rodin and of all artists... *The Thinker* is the artist, and he is thinking about art and life."

7 Elsen 1965, p. 70.

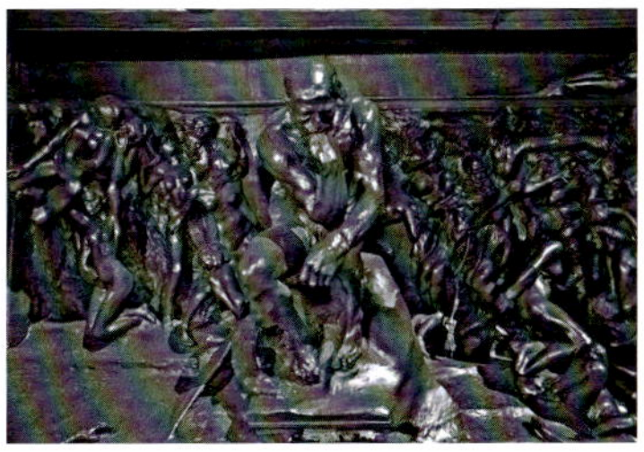

FIG.5A: Michelangelo Buonarotti, Il Pensiero, from the tomb of Lorenzo de' Medici, 1520–1534, marble, H. 70 in., Medici Chapel, San Lorenzo, Florence.

FIG. 5B: Grave of Auguste Rodin at Meudon.

FIG. 5C: Auguste Rodin, *The Thinker*, detail from *The Gates of Hell*, 1880–1900, Musée Rodin cast 1981, bronze, Iris and B. Gerald Cantor Center for Visual Arts, Stanford University, Gift of the B. Gerald Cantor Collection, 1985.86.

*"And the Dante, he that looks down upon hell…What could be more complete than this statue? This awful Thinker: seen from the left, he looks like a bird of prey contented with the vengeance he has meted out to the vile of the earth, a composition of physical and mental dominance, an effect of personality seemingly without a rival in all the sculpture of the world."*

TRUMAN BARTLETT

## 6 UGOLINO AND HIS SONS

Modeled 1881–1882, probably cast 1889
Bronze
16 1/8 × 16 7/8 × 19 7/8 in. (41 × 42.9 × 50.5 cm)
Gift of the Iris and B. Gerald Cantor Foundation, 2009 (2009.1.7)

*"Nothing is more frightening than Ugolino. Thin and wasted, his ribs jut against and through his skin; his empty listless mouth seems to foam like that of a famished wild animal upon contact with flesh. Like a hyena that has dug up carcasses, he crawls across the fallen bodies of his sons, whose inert arms and legs hang over into the abyss."*

OCTAVE MIRBEAU

Count Ugolino della Gherardesca was a powerful politician in thirteenth-century Pisa. The politics of the time were treacherous, and Ugolino was an adroit double-dealer who managed to stay in power for nearly seventeen eventful years, switching his allegiance between Guelph and Ghibelline factions. Eventually his own treachery led to his imprisonment in a tower, along with his sons and grandsons. They were held there for more than eight months and eventually starved to death. In Dante's *Inferno* (Cantos XXXII, 124–39; XXXIII, 1–87), the count was placed along with other traitors in the region of Antenora, in the ninth circle of hell. When Dante first encounters him, Ugolino is gnawing on his fellow traitor—and betrayer—Archbishop Ruggieri degli Ubaldini "at the place where brain is joined to neck" (Canto XXXII, 127–28). A few lines later Dante writes that as they neared death, Ugolino's children begged him to eat their bodies, and that eventually, for Ugolino, "starvation did what sorrow could not do" (Canto XXXIII, 61–75).

Though understandably a difficult subject for the public, the theme of Ugolino and his children was a popular one for nineteenth-century artists such as William Blake, Eugène Delacroix, and Gustave Doré. Rodin's predecessor Jean-Baptiste Carpeaux exhibited a pyramidal composition at the Salon of 1863 (FIG. 6A), which won a first-class medal and was later installed in the Tuileries Gardens, opposite a cast of the ancient statue of *Laocoön*. Rodin seems to have been especially drawn to the theme. After his return from Italy in 1876, he made a life-size torso of Ugolino and drew more than thirty sketches of the subject. By the following year, Rodin was modeling a seated version of Ugolino and included Ugolino and one of his sons in this upright format in his third maquette for *The Gates of Hell* (circa 1883). By 1889 Rodin's ideas for the group had evolved into one of the most complex multifigured compositions he had ever attempted. Ugolino had four sons and over three days watched them slowly die of starvation. Rodin depicts different stages of their poignant battle to survive. The two youngest (one an infant) have already succumbed. Another—barely alive—feebly tries to raise himself from the ground underneath his father, while the fourth weakly cries out as he struggles to pull himself up on his father's side. The bodies of the other three sons lie strewn around the exhausted, emaciated Ugolino, represented hollow-eyed and open-mouthed. His hunger and madness at having watched his sons die have reduced him to a pitiful, animal state. He crawls on his hands and knees, blindly grasping the head of one of his dead sons. As Ugolino describes himself in Dante's poem, "Now blind, I took to groping over each of them; and after they were dead, I called for them for two days" (Canto XXXIII, 73–75). As one writer described it, "There is let loose in him a terrible combat between the brute who wants to eat his fill and the thinking being, the loving being, who is horrified by such monstrous sacrilege. Nothing could be more poignant!"[1]

Rodin began exhibiting bronze casts that depicted the group in the round, and he inserted an abbreviated version into the center of the left door of *The Gates* (FIG. 6B). He continued to experiment with the composition after 1900, creating several groupings in which the poses and number of Ugolino's children varied significantly.

1 Gsell 1911, pp. 72–73.

Q "Auguste Rodin," *La France* (February 18, 1885), unpaginated.

FIG. 6A: Jean-Baptiste Carpeaux, *Ugolino and His Sons*, 1867, marble, H. 77 in., The Metropolitan Museum of Art, New York, purchase, Josephine Bay Paul and C. Michael Paul Foundation Inc., gift, and Charles Ulrock and Josephine Bay Foundation Inc., gift, and Fletcher Fund, 67.25.

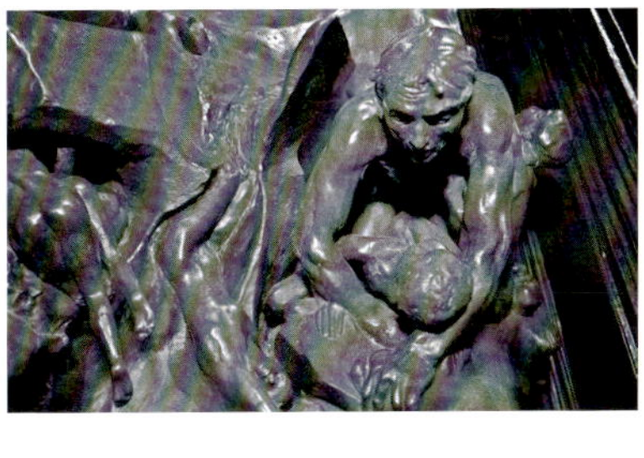

FIG. 6B: Auguste Rodin, *Ugolino and His Sons*, detail from *The Gates of Hell*, 1880–1900, Musée Rodin cast 1981, bronze, Iris and B. Gerald Cantor Center for Visual Arts, Stanford University, Gift of the B. Gerald Cantor Collection, 1985.86.

## 7 FALLEN CARYATID WITH A STONE

Modeled 1881–1882, enlarged 1911–1917, Musée Rodin cast 1988
Bronze
52 1/2 × 33 × 39 in. (133.4 × 83.8 × 99.1 cm)
Gift of the Iris and B. Gerald Cantor Foundation, 2009 (2009.1.8)

FIG. 7A: Greek, Erechtheion, 421–407 B.C.E., marble and limestone, Athens, Acropolis.

FIG. 7B: Auguste Rodin, *Fallen Caryatid with Urn*, modeled circa 1883, Musée Rodin cast 1967, bronze, 15 5/8 × 10 1/2 × 11 1/2 in., Iris and B. Gerald Cantor Center for Visual Arts, Stanford University, 1983.201.

In classical architecture caryatids are standing, draped female figures carved in columnar forms that serve as decorative supports (FIG. 7A). Rodin created two caryatids—one bearing a stone, the other an urn (FIG. 7B)—that differ radically from their classical predecessors. Instead of being erect, classically proportioned, and statuesque, Rodin's caryatids are compact, crouching nudes who appear crushed (or at least wearied and defeated), their physical strength unable to match their determination to bear their burdens. *Fallen Caryatid* is a graceful form, an ensemble of soft, flowing curves. The muscles of her back no longer strain against her burden; she has surrendered, collapsing under the unbearable weight of the stone. Rodin's inspiration for these figures derives from a passage in the *Inferno*, in which Dante strains to discern the nature of certain unidentifiable forms he sees in Hades. His guide, the Roman poet Virgil, explains they are the prideful, so bent under the stones they are condemned to eternally bear that they seem shapeless. One of them appears in the upper left corner of *The Gates of Hell*.

When Rodin exhibited a version of this work in 1886 among a group of sculptures titled *Weary Women*, the journalist Émile Michelet described it as "an admirable anatomy, expressing, through a creature crouching under a sidereal burden, the overwhelming oppression of sadness and despair, like the disillusion of having gazed too closely upon the mysteries of the stars that crush the foolhardy."[1] The figure bore an epigraph from one of Baudelaire's poems, "Le Guignon" ("Bad Luck"), from *The Flowers of Evil*, for which Rodin was working on a set of illustrations at the time: "Mainte fleur épanche à regret / Son parfum doux comme un secret / Dans les solitudes profondes. (And many a flower, to heal regret, / Pours forth its perfume as a secret / Amidst solitary shades.)" Michelet noted that the opening line of the poem ("To lift a weight so heavy would take your courage, Sisyphus!") was even more evocative of "the despair of this vibrant body, a caryatid from I don't know what mysterious, ineluctable archivolt."[2]

A more modern commentary on Rodin's *Fallen Caryatid with a Stone* appeared in Robert Heinlein's 1961 cult science fiction novel *Stranger in a Strange Land* (where Rodin's *Caryatid* appeared on the cover of the hardback first edition). There Jubal Harshaw, the "neo-pessimist philosopher," waxes eloquently about Rodin's sculpture: "This poor little caryatid has fallen under the load. She's a good girl—look at her face. Serious, unhappy at her failure, not blaming anyone, not even the gods ... and still trying to shoulder her load ... She's a symbol for every woman who ever shouldered a load too heavy. But not alone women—this symbol means every man and every woman who ever sweated out life in uncomplaining fortitude until they crumpled under their loads. It's courage ... and victory ... She's a father working while cancer eats away his insides, to bring home one more paycheck. She's a twelve-year-old trying to mother her brothers and sisters because mama had to go to Heaven ... She's all the unsung heroes who couldn't make it but never quit."[3]

1 *Jacques* (March 7, 1883), p. 3, in Le Normand-Romaine 2007, I, p. 247.

2 "Critique d'art. Le Salon de 1886," *Le Jeune France*, 8, 98 (July 1886), p. 772. Geffroy (1886, p. 1) described the stone the figure bears as "rounded, worn, immovable, and heavy like Unhappiness."

3 *Stranger in a Strange Land* (New York: Putnam, 1961) (ed. cit., 2003), p. 324.

A. Rodin

## 8 EVE (SMALL VERSION)

Modeled 1883, Musée Rodin cast 1967
Bronze
28 × 10 × 10 1/2 in. (71.1 × 25.4 × 26.7 cm)
Gift of the Iris and B. Gerald Cantor Foundation, 2009 (2009.1.9)

Rodin originally conceived of *Eve* to be paired with a matching figure of *Adam* to go on either side (or on top of) *The Gates of Hell*, like similar jamb figures flanking the entrance portals of Gothic cathedrals. His request to do so was refused, however, and his sculptures of Adam and Eve were realized and exhibited as independent figures apart from *The Gates*.

Nineteenth-century sculptors tended to represent Eve as a paragon of unspoiled, perfect beauty, tinged with both innocence and eroticism (FIG. 8A at left). Perhaps inspired by medieval and Renaissance depictions of the first couple being driven from the Garden of Eden, such as Michelangelo's *Expulsion from Eden* on the Sistine Chapel ceiling and Masaccio's fresco in the church of S. Maria del Carmine in Florence, Rodin instead sought to emphasize Eve's anguish over her role in the Fall. His *Eve* is crushed by the weight of her guilt: her head sinks downward in shame as she withdraws into the all-too-vulnerable shield of her arms. One hand (two fingers thrusting through her hair) hides her face from God's wrath, and the other remorsefully clutches her side. Every curve, joint, and muscle of her body expresses her despair and shame as she becomes aware of not only her sin but also her nakedness. Her soft flesh emphasizes her vulnerability.

Somewhat surprisingly, her belly protrudes slightly. Rodin related how he experienced some difficulty in modeling the figure: "Without knowing it, I saw my model changing. I modeled my contours, naïvely following the successive transformations of ever-amplifying form. One day I learned she was pregnant; then I understood. The contours of the belly had hardly changed; but you can see with what sincerity I copied nature in looking at the muscles of her loins and sides. It certainly hadn't occurred to me to take a pregnant model as my model for Eve; an accident—happy for me—gave her to me, and it aided the character of the figure singularly."[1] Rilke's awareness of this story colored his description of the work: "She bends forward as though listening over her own body in which a new future begins to stir. And it is as though the gravity of this future weighed upon the senses of the woman and drew her down from the freedom of life into the deep, humble service of motherhood."[2]

FIG. 8A: Jean Alexandre-Joseph Falguière, *Eve*, 1880, marble, H: 79 1/2 in., Ny Carlsberg Glyptotek, Copenhagen, inventory no. MIN 542.

1 Dujardin-Beaumetz 1913, in Elsen 1965, pp. 164–65.

2 Elsen 1965, p. 122.

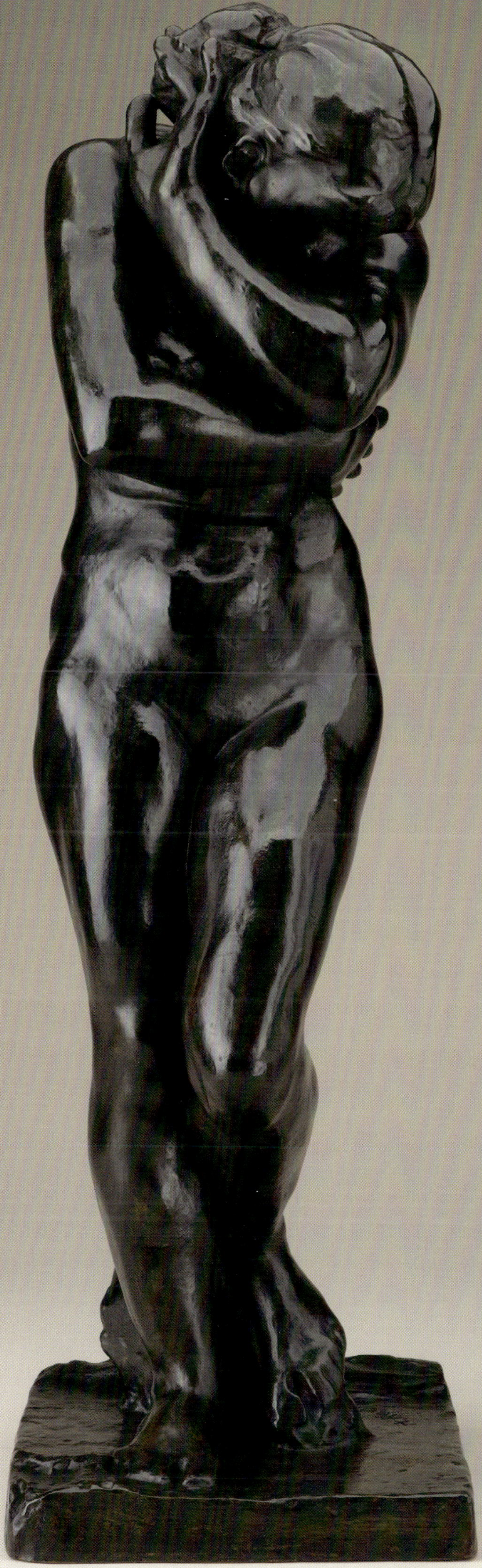

# 9 THE FALLING MAN

Modeled 1882, Musée Rodin cast 1979
Bronze
23 1/4 × 17 × 10 in. (59 × 43.2 × 25.4 cm)
Gift of the Iris and B. Gerald Cantor Foundation, 2009 (2009.1.10)

FIG. 9A: Auguste Rodin, *The Falling Man*, detail from *The Gates of Hell*, 1880–1900, Musée Rodin cast 1981, bronze, Iris and B. Gerald Cantor Center for Visual Arts, Stanford University, Gift of the B. Gerald Cantor Collection, 1985.86.

The acrobatic torsion and furrowed musculature of this figure led contemporary critics to identify it with various mythological characters: Marsyas, who was flayed alive by Apollo after having lost a musical competition to the god; Atlas, the primordial Titan condemned to bear the weight of the heavens on his shoulders; and Hercules, who temporarily took over Atlas's punishment in exchange for the Titan's help in securing the golden apples of the Hesperides.

*The Falling Man* must have been one of Rodin's favorite male forms to emerge from *The Gates of Hell* since it reappears throughout his oeuvre in many different incarnations. The present work has the appearance of a preliminary study, or at least of a work not intended to be viewed close up. The hair and eye sockets have been given only cursory treatment, and the torso has areas that are both smooth and hatched, suggesting the artist had not yet made up his mind as to which surface texture he preferred. Rodin left a lump of clay on the left leg (subsequently removed when the figure was reused in *I Am Beautiful* [CAT. 10]), while the barely finished hands were meant to be viewed only from the front, since the palms were left completely unarticulated. *The Falling Man* appears in three places on *The Gates*: clinging precariously to the lintel of the left door; as a single figure, posed upside down (FIG. 9A); and again on the right pilaster, combined with a female form, a group exhibited independently as *I Am Beautiful*. In 1885 Rodin added a different pair of arms and draped the figure with a large snake to create a unique sculpture (*Man with a Serpent*) for the collector Antony Roux. Although Roux insisted his was to be a unique cast, Rodin retained the right "to use the figure of the man but with modifications in the pose and without the serpent."[1]

Rodin exhibited *The Falling Man* independently in 1889 and 1900, and a truncated, headless variant of the sculpture may have been exhibited in 1904 under the title *Torso Louis XIV*. In 1900 Rodin combined it with yet another female figure to form *Group of Two Embracing Figures*. Elsen hypothesized that given the difficult, acrobatic pose of the figure, its model may have been the carnival strongman Cailloux, a Parisian street performer who was also the model for *Adam* and *The Three Shades* (CAT. 4).[2]

1 Le Normand-Romain 2007, II, p. 430, FIG. 2.

2 Elsen 2003, pp. 193, 248.

## 10 I AM BEAUTIFUL (JE SUIS BELLE)

Modeled circa 1885, cast at a later date (possibly 1918)
Bronze
27 3/4 × 12 × 12 1/2 in. (70.5 × 30.5 × 31.7 cm)
Gift of the Iris and B. Gerald Cantor Foundation, 2009 (2009.1.11)

The title comes from the opening lines of "Beauty" ("La Beauté"), Charles Baudelaire's poem about unreciprocated passion and emotional detachment. The opening lines of the poem, inscribed in French on the base of the sculpture, read:

Je suis belle, ô mortels! comme un rêve de pierre,
Et mon sein, où chacun s'est meurtri tour à tour,
Est fait pour inspirer au poète un amour
Éternel et muet ainsi que la matière.

FIG. 10A: Auguste Rodin, *The Crouching Woman*, circa 1880–1882, painted plaster, 12 1/2 × 10 × 7 in., Los Angeles County Museum of Art, Los Angeles, Gift of Iris and B. Gerald Cantor Foundation in honor of Vera Green, M.91.153.

This work is one of the earliest examples of the artist's revolutionary practice of combining independent figures to create new compositions. This was one of Rodin's most innovative and successful strategies, developed and refined during the twenty-year period he labored on *The Gates of Hell*. This process allowed Rodin to expand the repertoire of human forms he was creating and to explore the emotional nuances of those forms. In *I Am Beautiful*, he combined two sculptures, *The Crouching Woman* (FIG. 10A) and *The Falling Man* (CAT. 9), to create an extraordinary meditation on sexual desire and its complications.

Rodin said he was spontaneously inspired to create *The Crouching Woman* (nicknamed "The Frog") as he observed one of his favorite models, Adèle Abruzzezzi, unselfconsciously resting between posing sessions. The work does appear to be deliberately (or instinctively) composed, however. Contradictions abound within this figure, and these carry over into *I Am Beautiful*. Adèle's body creates a cube of compacted energy, yet the way her impossibly long right arm flows down and across so she can grasp her left foot creates a sinuous rhythm that dissipates this compacted energy. Her slumped shoulders and bent head suggest weariness and vulnerability, and she protectively covers her breast with her left hand. Yet at the same time her spread legs reveal—even flaunt—her sexuality.

Both figures are transformed in *I Am Beautiful*. The male is no longer the man who clings desperately to the lintel of *The Gates*. Energized by desire, he eagerly sweeps his would-be lover up into his arms. Joined for the first time (in low relief) on the right pilaster of *The Gates* (FIG. 10B), the couple is charged with an emotional fervor and tension absent from their individual identities. The American sculptor Truman Bartlett, who spent several days in Rodin's studio in late 1887, described the pair of figures as they appeared on *The Gates*: "A man holding to his breast and neck, with all the desperation of an undying love, the folded together form of a woman. The composition of this group is as original as the comprehension of the sentiment is fervid. It seems as though the spirit of a woman, in its haste to meet her lover, had shot through the air like a thought, to find rest in his arms. Neither figure seems fully conscious of the apparent effort of their bodies; it is something their hearts alone have done."[1]

Rodin created the group in the midst of his passionate, tormented affair with Camille Claudel. When first exhibited as an independent work, the sculpture was called *The Rape* (other titles given the piece include *Carnal Love* and *The Rut*), and its overt carnality caused a stir among critics: "No one has ever succeeded so well in expressing the savage onslaught of desire and the furious cries of the flesh," wrote Paul Guigou.[2]

A few years later, in 1889, the critic Gustave Geffroy wrote a particularly insightful description of *I Am Beautiful*: "The man stands, his feet planted in the ground, legs bent, his torso bent backwards under the strain, his head thrown back, holding in his arms, his fingers pressing into the flesh, a woman whose limbs are gathered together and joined in an angular, frog-like pose. She crouches, her chin touching her knees, her right hand grasps her left foot, the other pressed against her breast, all her bones protruding, all her flesh compressed into rigid folds. Lifted from the ground by the strong arms of the man, brought close to a heart and a face, she remains passive and mysterious. She is an unforgettable figure, whose coiled movement, tensed joints and back—branded as they are by the strain and rebellion of the flesh—are earthily animal, while her sorrowful face with closed eyes is tinged with an incurable sadness."[3]

As Geffroy's description suggests, for all its superficial joyfulness, *I Am Beautiful* reveals emotional complexities, even contradictions, that are as enigmatic as those Baudelaire expressed in his poem. Resting on her shoulder, the woman's turned head conveyed weariness in *The Crouching Woman*; here, turned away from the face of her would-be lover, it expresses rejection, underscored by her disdainful expression. Her right arm no longer grasps her left foot as it did in *The Crouching Woman*. Instead it hangs limply and together with her bent legs forms a passive barrier between the bodies. Compressed, she appears to withhold herself from the man's grasp,

FIG. 10B: Auguste Rodin, *I Am Beautiful*, detail from *The Gates of Hell*, 1880–1900, Musée Rodin cast 1981, bronze, Iris and B. Gerald Cantor Center for Visual Arts, Stanford University, Gift of the B. Gerald Cantor Collection, 1985.86.

coolly unyielding and emotionally detached, despite his intense desire. Perhaps Rodin was thinking of Camille, identifying her with Baudelaire's muse, upon whose breast "each man dies in his turn." Certainly he was sensitive to the mixed emotions that amorous relationships generate. As Geffroy wrote elsewhere about Rodin's couples: "The emotion expressed—even among the couples where bestial desire prevails, where lovers are joined—is always profound and mournful. Rodin is the sculptor of sorrowful lust."[4] The contradictions extend into the physical realm as well. Is the male figure straining under the weight of the female, or triumphantly lifting her up? The woman's crouched pose expresses both dense mass and upward buoyancy. In the final analysis, the conflicting emotions, contradictions, and enigmas expressed in Rodin's sculpture are as profound and complex as those in any intense personal relationship.

*La Beauté*

Je suis belle, ô mortels! comme un rêve de pierre,
Et mon sein, où chacun s'est meurtri tour à tour,
Est fait pour inspirer au poète un amour
Éternel et muet ainsi que la matière.

Je trône dans l'azur comme un sphinx incompris;
J'unis un cœur de neige à la blancheur des cygnes;
Je hais le mouvement qui déplace les lignes,
Et jamais je ne pleure et jamais je ne ris.

Les poètes, devant mes grandes attitudes,
Que j'ai l'air d'emprunter aux plus fiers monuments,
Consumeront leurs jours en d'austères études;

Car j'ai pour fasciner ces dociles amants,
De purs miroirs qui font les étoiles plus belles:
Mes yeux, mes larges yeux aux clartés éternelles!

—Charles Baudelaire

*Beauty*

I am beautiful, O mortals! like a dream in stone,
And my breast, where each one in turn has bruised himself,
Is made to inspire in the poet a love
Eternal and silent as matter.

An unfathomable sphinx, I hold court in the sky;
I join my heart of snow to the whiteness of swans;
I hate motion that supplants line,
And never do I weep and never do I laugh.

Poets, before my grandiose poses,
Which I appear to assume from the proudest statues,
Will consume their days in austere study;

For I have, to enchant those docile lovers,
Pure mirrors that make the stars more beautiful:
My wide, wide eyes, eternally bright![5]

1 Bartlett 1889, in Elsen 1965, p. 73. Bartlett's own drawing of the group served as one of the illustrations that accompanied his account.

2 *Revue moderniste* 8 (September 30, 1885), p. 74, in Lampert 1986, p. 205.

3 Geffroy 1889, pp. 65–66, reprinted in Monet-Rodin 1889/1989, pp. 63–64.

4 Geffroy 1886, p. 1.

5 Charles Baudelaire, "Beauty," from *The Flowers of Evil*. Much of this translation is borrowed from William Aggeler's *The Flowers of Evil* (Fresno, Calif.: Academy Library Guild, 1954), but I have retranslated a few lines, incorporating suggestions from my colleagues Joseph Covington and Caroline Rocheleau, and from Professor Elizabeth Barron at Wake Forest University. I am grateful for their assistance.

## 11 THE KISS

Modeled circa 1881–1882, cast at a later date
Bronze
34 × 17 × 22 in. (86.4 × 43.2 × 55.9 cm)
Gift of the Iris and B. Gerald Cantor Foundation, 2009 (2009.1.12)

The story of the ill-fated lovers Paolo and Francesca is one of the most poignant episodes recounted by Dante in *The Divine Comedy* (*Inferno*, Canto V, 97–138) and one of the few subjects drawn directly from the poem that remained on *The Gates*. Francesca, the daughter of Count Giovanni da Polenta of Rimini, was betrothed about 1275 to Gianciotto Malatesta, eldest son of the lord of Rimini. However, she fell in love with Gianciotto's younger brother, Paolo, who was her tutor, and whom Dante knew personally. When Dante encounters her in the *Inferno*, Francesca explains how the couple's love began innocently "One day while reading for pleasure / about Lancelot and how love had overcome him. / We were alone and unsuspecting, / And time and time again that passage led our eyes to meet, / and took the color from our faces. / But there was only one passage that overcame us. / When as we read of the much-longed-for smile / Being by such a noble lover kissed / he who shall never be parted from me, tremblingly kissed me on the mouth...that day we read no farther" (Canto V, 127–38). The lovers were discovered at the moment of their embrace by Francesca's fiancé, who killed them both. Dante placed Paolo and Francesca in the second circle of hell, condemned to be forever swept along on the wind with other carnal sinners who "sinned within the flesh, subjecting reason to the rule of lust" (Canto V, 38–39).

The story of Paolo and Francesca was a popular one in nineteenth-century art, but Rodin, who depicted it numerous times, chose to treat the theme very differently from his contemporaries.[1] Aristide Croisy's interpretation (FIG. 11A) of the same moment in the story was carved less than a decade before Rodin's *The Kiss*. Croisy's version is true to Dante's narrative. Here the couple is young, innocent, and fully clothed, but the sculpture hardly rises above mere illustration. Rodin's Paolo and Francesca are adults, nude, and no longer innocent. Rodin inserts an element of tension between the two figures. Paolo is the more hesitant of the two, as if mindful of the fact his brother is his lover's fiancé. His back is stiff and tense, the touch of his right hand tentative. Francesca is more assertive. Her eyes are rapturously shut, while his are just beginning to close as he surrenders to her (and his) passion. Her leg is slung over Paolo's thigh, while the toes of her left foot gently caress his; her body leans into his in a sinuous reverse *S* curve as she draws his head to hers. The figures' lips barely meet in the moment in which the hesitant Paolo yields completely to Francesca's passionate embrace.

The only suggestion of a connection to Dante's story is the book that slips from Paolo's left hand—one of the rare instances the artist provides a narrative detail (cf. *St. John the Baptist Preaching* [CAT. 3]; the water jug beside the Danaïd [CAT. 12] is another). But this detail is barely noticeable, and Rodin's decision to represent his figures in the nude removes any reference to a specific time and place. He was determined to make a universal statement about physical desire and passion, and a new naturalistic approach to the nude, one not bound by references to classical mythology or the antique. It is a measure of his artistic skill and creativity that he could do so, taking as his inspiration and point of departure a brief episode from a fourteenth-century poem.

Rodin intended *The Kiss* to show the official art world he could compose with the best academic sculptors of his day, and it was one of his few works to receive critical praise when it was first exhibited. One of the best descriptions came from Gustave Geffroy, who wrote, "The man's head is bent, that of the woman is lifted, and their mouths meet in a kiss that seals the intimate union of their two beings. Through the extraordinary magic of art, this kiss, which is scarcely indicated by the meeting of their lips, is clearly visible, not only in their meditative expressions, but still more in the shiver that runs equally through both bodies, from the nape of the neck to the soles of the feet, in every fiber of the man's back, as it bends, straightens, grows still, where everything adores—bones, muscles, nerves, flesh—in his leg, which seems to twist slowly, as if moving to brush against his lover's leg; and in the woman's feet, which hardly touch the ground, uplifted with her whole being as she is swept away with ardor and grace."[2]

FIG. 11A: Aristide Croisy, *Paolo and Francesca*, 1876, plaster, 59 × 40 ½ × 29 ½ in., Musée de l'Ardenne et Musée Arthur Rimbaud, Charleville-Mézières.

1 Bordeaux 1975.

2 Monet-Rodin 1889/1989, pp. 64–65. When exhibited at the Chicago World's Fair of 1893, *The Kiss* was deemed so scandalously erotic that it was placed in a room that could be visited only by special permission.

## (12) DANAÏD

Modeled 1885–1889, Musée Rodin cast 1979
Bronze
12 3/4 × 28 3/4 × 22 1/2 in. (32.4 × 73 × 57.2 cm)
Gift of the Iris and B. Gerald Cantor Foundation, 2009 (2009.1.13)

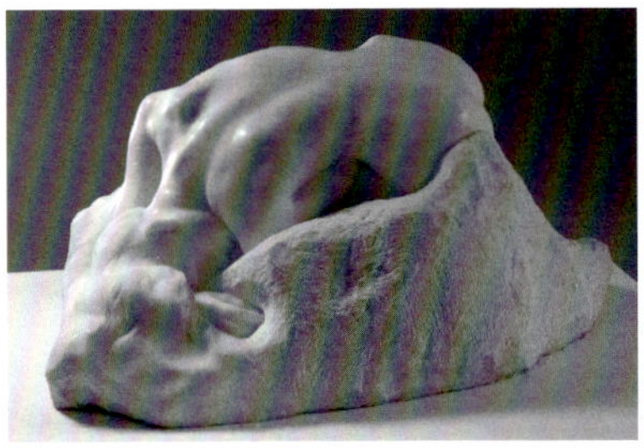

FIG. 12A: Auguste Rodin, *Danaïd*, 1889–1890, marble, 14 1/7 × 27 1/2 × 21 1/4 in., Musée Rodin, Paris, S. 1155.

There are differing accounts in classical literature of the Danaïdes, the fifty daughters of King Danaos of Argos. He had promised them in marriage to the fifty sons of his brother Aegyptos, but then the two brothers became enemies. Danaos and his daughters fled to Argos to flee Aegyptos's wrath. Eventually the fifty sons came to Argos to propose marriage to the Danaïdes as a conciliatory gesture, but the vengeful Danaos ordered his daughters to murder their bridegrooms on their wedding night. All but one of them obeyed. According to later classical authors, the Danaïdes were condemned to Hades for their crimes, and their unending penance was to fill leaking vessels with water. Although the story was not recounted in Dante's *Inferno*, it seems probable Rodin originally intended *Danaïd* for *The Gates of Hell* as yet another example of the human suffering that results from human passions. Ultimately, however, he decided not to incorporate the figure into *The Gates.*

Rodin represents a single Danaïd, overcome by exhaustion and despair at her eternal fate. Her fatigue and desolation have brought her to her knees, as she collapses upon the rock, which the form of her body mimics. Rodin achieves an extraordinary intensity of expression through the pose and attitude of the Danaïd's body. As Elsen wrote, "With *Danaïd* ... Rodin was claiming that he could make a woman's back as expressive as her face."[1]

It is one of the artist's most sensual and beautifully modeled anatomies, an ensemble of graceful lines, volumes, and contrasting surface textures. The torsion of the girl's pose emphasizes the soft curves and hollows of her upper body and arm, which contrast strikingly with the craggy surface of the rock. Her flowing tresses mimic the water that spills from the cracked, overturned vessel beneath her on the other side.

The beautiful surface qualities of the bronze led to an immediate demand for marble versions (FIG. 12A), of which at least five examples exist, one of them included in the 1889 *Monet-Rodin* exhibition, where it received considerable critical praise. Speaking of a marble version, Rilke described *Danaïd* as "a figure that has thrown itself from a kneeling position down into a wealth of flowing hair. Simply walking around this marble creates a marvelous impression, following the long, very long line that curves around the generously unfolding roundness of the back, toward the face, which loses itself in the stone like a great weeping, and toward the hand, which like a broken flower once more speaks softly of the life that lies deep within the heart of the stone."[2]

*"With the Danaïde—a marvelous piece of shimmering flesh, shaped in light—[we see] the human soul's despair before the ever-unfinished labor, the inconsolable regret for the unrealizeable dream, the impotence of the finite before the infinite."*

FÉLIX JEANTET

1 Elsen 2003, p. 505.

2 Elsen 1965, p. 129.

Q "Exposition des œuvres de Rodin," *Le Blanc et Noir* (June 1889), reprinted in Monet-Rodin 1889/1989, pp. 232–33.

# 13 TOILETTE OF VENUS AND ANDROMEDA

Modeled after 1890, Musée Rodin cast 1987
Bronze
20 × 14 1/2 × 23 1/2 in. (50.8 × 36.8 × 59.7 cm)
Gift of the Iris and B. Gerald Cantor Foundation, 2009 (2009.1.14)

Rodin created this assemblage by combining two previously independent pieces: *Andromeda*, a marble carved in 1885, from which the mold for the bronze was made, and *Toilette of Venus*, modeled about 1890 (FIG. 13A). The latter figure is closely related to two other sculptures Rodin was working on at the time, *Kneeling Fauness* (FIG. 13B) and *The Awakening*, as well as a drawing he made as an illustration to Baudelaire's poem "Le Guignon" (FIG. 13C).

The piece appears to have been somewhat haphazardly assembled from two crude models for *Andromeda* and *Toilette of Venus* that were left in Rodin's studio. Neither figure has been carefully finished. Bits of clay debris that are not found on the single bronze figure of Andromeda appear on her leg and torso in the assemblage. Venus's hair, which was modeled with more care in the independent figure, is a barely articulated lump in the combined work, abruptly truncated when the artist removed a chunk of clay from the model. Visible seams have been left along the sides of her body. There is no obvious narrative or iconographic connection between Venus and the Ethiopian princess Andromeda, and equally little direct link between the two sculptures and their mythological counterparts. What may have inspired Rodin to bring together the two figures is the contrasting ways their poses express the inherent energy contained in the human body. The figure of Andromeda—closely related to Rodin's *Danaïd* (CAT. 12), particularly in the modeling of her back—is compacted, wedded to its rocky support, which has been abruptly tilted upward. The form's energy is contained in as small an area as possible. The upright figure of Venus releases her energy as she arches her back and stretches her torso. It is almost as if the somnolent figure of Andromeda has risen from her slumber and stretches as she awakens.

FIG. 13A: Auguste Rodin, *Toilette of Venus*, circa 1885–1886, bronze, 18 × 9 ½ × 8 ½ in., Iris and B. Gerald Cantor Collection, Promised gift to the Iris and B. Gerald Cantor Foundation, inventory no. 126000.

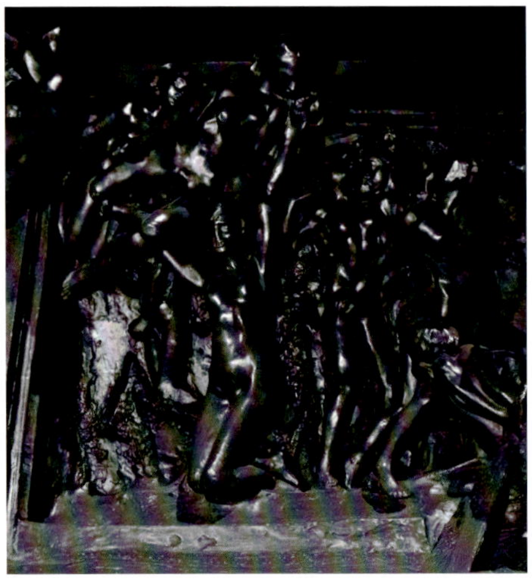

FIG. 13B: Auguste Rodin, *Kneeling Fauness*, detail from *The Gates of Hell*, 1880–1900, Musée Rodin cast 1981, bronze, Iris and B. Gerald Cantor Center for Visual Arts, Stanford University, Gift of the B. Gerald Cantor Collection, 1985.86.

XI

LE GUIGNON

Pour soulever un poids si lourd,
Sisyphe, il faudrait ton courage!
Bien qu'on ait du cœur à l'ouvrage,
L'Art est long et le Temps est court.

Loin des sépultures célèbres,
Vers un cimetière isolé,
Mon cœur, comme un tambour voilé,
Va battant des marches funèbres.

— Maint joyau dort enseveli
Dans les ténèbres et l'oubli,
Bien loin des pioches et des sondes;

Mainte fleur épanche à regret
Son parfum doux comme un secret
Dans les solitudes profondes.

FIG. 13C: Auguste Rodin, *Le Guignon*, 1887–1888, pen and ink drawing reproduced in Charles Baudelaire's *Les Fleurs du mal*, 1918 (Paris: The Limited Editions Club, 1940).

## 14 FUGITIVE LOVE (FUGIT AMOR)

Modeled before 1887, cast at a later date (1930–1951?)
Bronze
20 3/4 × 33 × 15 in. (52.7 × 83.8 × 38.1 cm)
Gift of the Iris and B. Gerald Cantor Foundation, 2009 (2009.1.15)

Rodin created this group by combining the figure of *The Prodigal Son*—who in turn derives from one of the sons in the Ugolino group (CAT. 6)—with that of a woman whose back and head are uplifted and arched like a ship's masthead as she blithely glides along the wind. The gracefully fluid pair was known by many names—*Course to the Abyss, The Sphinx, The Dream, The Chimera, Night, Dawn*—but the group is now most commonly known as *Fugit Amor* (*Fugitive Love*, literally "love flees"). The work probably has its origins in the tempest-borne adulterers described in Dante's second circle of hell (*Inferno*, Canto V), although it should probably not be understood as representing a specific pair of lovers, rather those "for whom no hope ever comforts, no hope for rest and none for lesser pain" (Canto V, 44–45). In this respect the work epitomizes the mood of desperation and tormenting lack of fulfillment that permeates *The Gates of Hell*, where the pair appears twice on the right portal, arranged both horizontally and vertically, surging upward and outward from the surrounding chaos (FIG. 14A). These two variants on *The Gates* and the independent composition enabled the artist to fully mine the expressive potential of the group. *Fugitive Love* seems to have enjoyed considerable popularity, as numerous bronzes exist and at least four marble copies are known.

FIG. 14A: Auguste Rodin, *Fugitive Love*, detail from *The Gates of Hell*, 1880–1900, Musée Rodin cast 1981, bronze, Iris and B. Gerald Cantor Center for Visual Arts, Stanford University, Gift of the B. Gerald Cantor Collection, 1985.86.

The woman below eludes the grasp of the male, whose thin, adolescent body stretches above hers, back to back, as he longingly reaches for her. She looks straight ahead, her lips tightly compressed, her expression grim and impassive as the Sphinx. Unmoved by his desperation and need, she flies from him as he groans in anguished frustration, denied the union he desperately (and futilely) seeks. The upper half of the man's body strains to grasp the fleeing woman, as if attempting to hold onto a love no longer reciprocated, while his legs dangle limply behind him. As though fusing Dante's eternally frustrated lovers and the bitter souls described in Baudelaire's poetry, Rodin's sculpture expresses man's inability to comprehend woman—literally and physically—and the cruelty and anguish of unrequited love. The earliest title of the work, *Course to the Abyss*, suggests the woman is a means to a man's downfall, while other early titles, *The Sphinx* and *The Chimera*, suggest she is a dangerous, enigmatic creature, a *femme fatale*. All of these ideas are prevalent themes in nineteenth-century symbolist literature and poetry. An 1899 description of the pair by the critic Gabriel Mourey follows this line: "*The Chimera* shows a woman with [a] cold, indifferent, impassive face, her eyes looking straight ahead. She is bearing away in her flight the poet captured by her fascinations. He clings to her, and frail as she is, her strength is enough to carry him off. His face drawn with half-voluptuous pain, he gazes on her yearningly, as if to fathom the enigma of her being, and his body writhes in torture. But she flies along, listless and disdainful, her lips smiling with a smile of victorious witchery."[1] If *I Am Beautiful* (CAT. 10) expresses the torment of unrequited passion in response to the first expression of desire, then *Fugitive Love*, as the French novelist and critic Paul Bourget noted, "is the whole symbol ... of the terrible struggles that accompany the ends of love."[2]

*"All of Rodin's art is in this small bronze, more sorrowful than anything in Baudelaire's poems. Her upper torso stretched upward, thrusting breasts ripe with tempting flesh, horizontal body quivering like an arrow splitting the air, and cruel, inexorable face, the woman is borne through space. She has that unembraceable beauty of the chimeras we pursue and the dreams we shall never realize."*

OCTAVE MIRBEAU

1 "The Work of Auguste Rodin," *The Studio,* XIII, 62 (May 1898), p. 221, in DeCaso and Sanders 1973, p. 165.

2 *Physiologie de l'amour moderne,* "Meditation XIV. De la Rupture I," *La vie parisienne* (June 18, 1889), republished in book form (Paris: Alphonse Lemerre, 1891), p. 273.

Q "Auguste Rodin," *L'Écho de Paris* (June 25, 1899), p. 1, reprinted in Monet-Rodin 1889/1989, p. 226.

## 15 SORROW

Modeled circa 1888–1889, Musée Rodin cast 1983
Bronze
11 1/2 × 6 1/2 × 6 3/4 in. (29.2 × 16.5 × 17.1 cm)
Gift of the Iris and B. Gerald Cantor Foundation, 2009 (2009.1.16)

Sorrow is one of the principal themes of *The Gates of Hell*, so it is surprising this figure only made its way onto *The Gates* in the final state, where it appears as an independent standing figure in the upper right corner of the right door. A female figure with her face hidden in her arms was often used as an allegory of grief, a motif frequently encountered in funerary sculpture. At one point Rodin's *Sorrow* was exhibited under the title *Figure for a Tomb*.[1]

In 1900 the figure was exhibited in a horizontal position, lying face down. Rodin subsequently combined this version of *Sorrow* with another single figure, *Reclining Woman*, to create the work known as *The Dream*. *Sorrow* was not cast in bronze as an independent figure until 1983. The figure is modeled with its rocky background, which serves to isolate the figure and hide her face, allowing the viewer to imagine her pained expression.

In 1998 the Musée Rodin selected *Sorrow* to be used in an educational model demonstrating the different stages involved in the lost-wax casting process (FIG. 15A). One of these models was included in the Cantor Foundation gift to the North Carolina Museum of Art.

FIG. 15A: Ten-step lost-wax casting process of *Sorrow*, 1987, 10 pieces, each approx. 10 × 4 ½ × 5 in., North Carolina Museum of Art, Raleigh, Gift of the Iris and B. Gerald Cantor Foundation.

1 Carl Burckhardt, *Rodin und das plastische Problem* (Basel: Benno Schwabe & Co., Basler Kunstverein, 1921), p. 84, pl. 45, in Le Normand-Romain 2007, I, p. 311.

## 16 FLYING FIGURE

Modeled circa 1890–1891, enlarged circa 1900, Musée Rodin cast 1981
Bronze
20 1/2 × 29 1/2 × 12 in. (52.1 × 74.9 × 30.5 cm)
Gift of the Iris and B. Gerald Cantor Foundation, 2009 (2009.1.17)

*Flying Figure* is one of the most eloquent testimonies to Rodin's revolutionary practice of seeking the essential qualities of an idea he wished to express in sculpture by paring down the work and removing the features he deemed extraneous, distilling the figure until what remained was the purest expression of what he wished to reveal. The figure can be traced to the female form in an earlier sculpture, *Avarice and Lust*, which Rodin created about 1881–84 (FIG. 16A) and subsequently added to *The Gates of Hell*.[1] It is not known for certain whether *Flying Figure* derived directly from the earlier form, or whether Rodin was inspired to create it from a live model posing before him.[2] The fragmentary torso and splayed legs of *Flying Figure*, as well as its kinetic energy, anticipate Rodin's *Iris* (FIG. 16B).

Whether Rodin started with the earlier form or a live model, it is clear that as soon as he was done modeling the figure, he began paring it down: the head; nearly the entire left leg, leaving only a stump of the upper thigh to support her; the lower half of her left arm; and the right foot. The right hand grasps her thigh, creating a sleek, aerodynamic silhouette.

In contrast to the softly modeled surface of the figure's torso, her back is a tableau of violent activity, perhaps brought about by the artist's desire to imbue the figure with greater aerodynamism. A substantial portion of her back has been slashed away; the intensity of this action is indicated by the ridges of clay forced outward and downward as the blade was pressed into the model in curving sweeps. Chunks of clay were also removed from the calf of the right leg and (to a considerably lesser degree) from her right elbow. The overall effect of the violence done to the clay model is at once shocking and hauntingly beautiful. In Rodin's own day, it must have appeared even more shocking. The American sculptor Frederick Ruckstall may have had *Flying Figure* in mind when he wrote in 1925:

"But why any man should, today, *deliberately model* a human body and then *mutilate it* and *hack it*, and exhibit it, except as a revelation of his sadistic soul, passes our comprehension. The first man, as far as we know, to do this was Rodin—who was regarded in Paris, as a moral sot."[3]

What remains is an intangible idea—energy, motion, trajectory—given essential form. Rodin himself discussed how his ideas about movement had evolved: "I used to think that movement was the chief thing in sculpture, and in all I did it was what I tried to attain... I have come to gradually feel that sculptural expression is the essence of the statuary art—expression through the modeling. This is what made the grandeur of the Greeks."[4] Critic Leo Steinberg remarked that in *Flying Figure*, "Rodin has not so much modeled a body in motion, as clothed a motion in body, and in no more body than it wants to fulfill itself... the sculpture represents an energy—like an electrical discharge in a lightning rod—which has found a conductor body."[5]

FIG. 16A: Auguste Rodin, *Avarice and Lust*, circa 1881–1884, bronze, 8 1/2 × 20 1/2 × 16 1/2 in., Iris and B. Gerald Cantor Center for Visual Arts, Stanford University, Gift of the Iris and B. Gerald Cantor Foundation, 1975.184.

FIG. 16B: Auguste Rodin, *Iris, Messenger of the Gods*, modeled 1890–1900, Musée Rodin cast 1966, bronze, 31 × 35 × 14 in., Los Angeles County Museum of Art, Gift of B. Gerald Cantor Art Foundation, M.73.108.11.

1 *Avarice and Lust* was created by combining two distinct figures. The male figure was constructed using the upper half of *The Falling Man* (CAT. 9), repositioning the arms, and adding a new head. The female figure probably had its origins in one of the plaster models for the hovering figures who appear in the upper left tympanum of *The Gates*. It also relates to another sculpture, *The Martyr*, which in turn relates to a drawing Rodin used to illustrate Baudelaire's poem "A Carrion," from *The Flowers of Evil*. When *Avarice and Lust* was added to *The Gates*, the group was turned on its side, so the woman's body faces outward.

2 Le Normand-Romain (2007, I, p. 370) suggests the female figure was cut from a clay model for *Avarice and Lust* using a wire while the clay was still wet. While *Flying Figure* bears striking similarities to this earlier figure, I am inclined to follow Elsen's view (2003, p. 573) that *Flying Figure* was based on a pose by a live model in the studio; in any case a plaster of *Avarice and Lust* was in Rodin's studio at the time he created *Flying Figure*.

3 Ruckstall 1925, p. 23.

4 Lawton 1906, pp. 160–61.

5 Steinberg 1972, p. 363.

*"Rodin has not so much modeled a body in motion, as clothed a motion in body, and in no more body than it wants to fulfill itself... the sculpture represents an energy—like an electrical discharge in a lightning rod—which has found a conductor body."*

LEO STEINBERG

# THE BURGHERS OF CALAIS

In 1884, while he was still intensely involved with *The Gates of Hell*, Rodin was approached by the city of Calais to submit designs for a monument commemorating a celebrated episode in its history. This episode was very briefly recounted in the fourteenth-century *Chronicles* of Jean Froissart, which covered the history of Western Europe during the fourteenth century. In 1347, during the Hundred Years' War, the English King Edward III laid siege to the French city of Calais for eleven months, and its citizens were on the verge of starvation. The king agreed to lift the siege and spare the city from annihilation if six of the chief burghers of Calais would come out of the town "bare-headed, barefooted, and bare-legged, and in their shirts, with halters about their necks; with the keys of the town and castle in their hands, and let them six yield themselves purely to my will." According to Froissart, six of the city's most prominent citizens agreed to do so.

Soon afterward the richest burgher in the town, Sir Eustace de Saint-Pierre, got up and said, "Gentlemen, it would be a great shame to allow so many people to starve to death, if there were any way of preventing it. And it would be highly pleasing to Our Lord if anyone could save them such a fate. I have such faith in gaining pardon and grace from Our Lord if I die in the attempt, that I will put myself forward as the first. I will willingly go out in my shirt, bare-headed and barefoot, with a halter around my neck and put myself at the mercy of the King of England."[1]

Another very rich and much respected citizen, Jean d'Aire, rose and said he would keep Sir Eustace company. The third to volunteer was Sir Jacques de Wissant, wealthy both by inheritance and by his own transactions. De Wissant offered to accompany his two cousins, and so did Sir Pierre, his brother. Two others completed the number and set off dressed only in their shirts and breeches, with halters around their necks, as they had been told.

The six burghers undoubtedly believed that entering Edward's camp and submitting themselves to the king's will would result in their deaths. Rodin portrayed them walking out of the city to meet their grim fate, each preoccupied with his own conflicting emotions. Since the citizens of Calais had caused so many of his own men to die, the English king was inclined to hang the hostages, despite the entreaties of his own knights, who were moved by the courage of the six burghers. It was only after the queen begged him to spare their lives that he reluctantly agreed to do so.

In autumn 1884 Rodin submitted a maquette (model) (CAT. 17) to the town council of Calais. In the maquette the artist arranged the six figures in a compact cube, linked by a rope and elevated on a pedestal. On the basis of this model, the council approved the selection of Rodin for the project but ordered him to complete a second maquette, one-third the final size. Rodin probably submitted this maquette (FIG. 16) to the council in July 1885. They criticized both Rodin's design and his less-than-heroic presentation of the figures: "This is not the way we envisaged our glorious citizens going to the camp of the King of England. Their defeated postures offend our religion ...We feel it our duty to insist that M. Rodin modify the attitudes of his figures and the silhouette of the group."[2] Rodin eventually overcame the council's objections and worked on the monument over the next four years. He separately modeled heads, torsos, hands, and feet, as well as the figures themselves (both in the nude and clothed), combining and recombining them until he was satisfied.

"I have not shown them grouped in a triumphant apotheosis; such a glorification of their heroism would not have corresponded to anything real. On the contrary, I have, as it were, strung them one behind the other, because in the indecision of the final inner combat which arises between their devotion to their city and their fear of dying, each of them is isolated in front of his conscience. They are still questioning themselves to know if they have the strength to accomplish the supreme sacrifice... Their soul pushes them onward, and yet their feet refuse to walk."

FIG. 15: Auguste Rodin, *The Burghers of Calais, First Maquette* (detail), CAT. 17.

FIG. 16: Auguste Rodin, *The Burghers of Calais, Second Maquette*, modeled July 1885, Musée Rodin cast 1971, bronze, composed of six separate, free-standing figures, H. approx. 27 in. each, Iris and B. Gerald Cantor Center for Visual Arts at Stanford University, Gift of the Iris and B. Gerald Cantor Foundation, 1974.98–103.

In 1889 a life-size plaster model for the work was unveiled at a Paris exhibition devoted to Rodin and Claude Monet. After several years of delay owing to difficulties raising the funds required to cast the group in bronze, the final monument was unveiled to the public in Calais on June 3, 1895. *The Burghers of Calais* (FIG. 17) represents a turning point in the history of the public monument. Rodin represented his figures not as heroes, as Froissart portrayed them and as his artistic predecessors had done, but as vulnerable human beings united in a moment of truth, bound to each other and to a fate each has freely chosen out of a sense of civic duty, but which nevertheless has caused each of them considerable emotional turmoil. As Rodin explained, "I have not shown them grouped in a triumphant apotheosis; such a glorification of their heroism would not have corresponded to anything real. On the contrary, I have, as it were, strung them one behind the other, because in the indecision of the final inner combat which arises between their devotion to their city and their fear of dying, each of them is isolated in front of his conscience. They are still questioning themselves to know if they have the strength to accomplish the supreme sacrifice...Their soul pushes them onward, and yet their feet refuse to walk."[3]

1 Joliffe 1967, p. 155. All comments by Froissart appear on p. 155.

2 Tancock 1976, p. 383; Tancock's essay (pp. 376–95) on the commission is exemplary.

The most thorough study on the project is McNamara and Elsen 1977; also see Elsen 2003, pp. 65–92.

3 Paul Gsell, "Chez Rodin," *Rodin: L'Homme et l'oeuvre, L'Art et les artistes*, vol. 19, no. 109 (April 1914), pp. 66–67, trans. Tancock 1976, pp. 388–89, 395, n. 26.

Q Gsell 1914, pp. 67–68; Tancock 1976, pp. 385, 394, n. 23.

**FIG. 17:** Auguste Rodin, *The Burghers of Calais,* modeled 1884–1895, Musée Rodin cast 1985, bronze, 82 ½ × 94 × 95 in., The Metropolitan Museum of Art, New York, Gift of Iris and B. Gerald Cantor, 1989.407.

*"I did not want any pedestal for these statues. I wanted them to be placed on, even affixed to, the paving stones of the public square in front of the Hôtel de Ville in Calais, so that it looked as if they were leaving there in order to go out to the enemy camp. In this way they would have been, as it were, mixed with the daily life of the town: passersby would have elbowed them, and they would have felt keenly through this contact the emotion of the living past in their midst; they would have said to themselves: 'Our ancestors are our neighbors and our models, and the day when it will be granted to us to imitate their example, we would show that we have not degenerated from their virtue!'"*

## 17 THE BURGHERS OF CALAIS, FIRST MAQUETTE

Modeled 1884, Musée Rodin cast 1987
Bronze
23 3/4 × 14 7/8 × 13 in. (60.3 × 37.7 × 33 cm)
Gift of the Iris and B. Gerald Cantor Foundation, 2009 (2009.1.18)

In a letter dated November 20, 1884, Rodin described his initial maquette to the mayor of Calais: "The idea seems to me to be completely original from the point of view of architecture and sculpture. Furthermore, it is the subject itself that is [original], and imposes a heroic conception: the group of six figures offering themselves to an internal experience, to an expressive emotion. The pedestal is triumphal and has the rudiments of a triumphal arch to carry, not a quadriga [a chariot and horses], but human patriotism, self-denial, and virtue... Rarely have I succeeded in giving a sketch such élan and sobriety."[1]

Sculptors earlier elected to represent only the figure of Eustache de St. Pierre, or to accord him greater prominence, and the Municipal Council of Calais had envisioned the project as "The Devotion of Eustache de St. Pierre and His Companions."[2] Rodin decided to give each of the six nearly equal prominence from the outset, according Eustache slightly more emphasis through his bold gesture and by virtue of the fact that he holds the large key to the city. In this, the artist's initial model for the project, he arranged the six figures in a tightly packed cube, three facing out from one side, two from the opposite side, and the sixth at one end, so the group would be effective from different viewpoints. Along the front side of the maquette, one of the burghers (Pierre de Wissant?) gestures inwardly with his right hand as if questioning himself. His left arm rests on the shoulders of one of his comrades (perhaps his brother Jacques, since he is represented with a beard, as he is in the final model), whose neck is also encircled by a rope halter. That comrade in turn holds onto Eustache de St. Pierre, the leader of the group, who points the way out of the city with his left arm. On the far right, the figure of Andrieu d'Andres bends over in anguish, the forward thrust of his body echoing the curve of Eustache's arm and relieving the more upright poses of the other figures. On the other side of the model, two figures (one of them youthful in appearance, so he may perhaps be Jean de Fiennes) grasp hands as they break their farewell embrace.

On the strength of this model, the Municipal Council of Calais offered Rodin the commission for the monument, although it stipulated he create a second model for approval. In the latter work, Rodin abandoned the triumphal arch composition and intertwined figures of the first maquette for a group of six more independent figures standing at eye level on a low rise of ground. This was the compositional strategy he would retain in the final monument.

1 Tancock 1976, pp. 382, 393, n. 12.

2 In 1849 the sculptor Louis Rochet proposed a monument that would represent St. Pierre on a pedestal with five smaller figures below representing the other burghers. In his model Émile Chatrousse, another candidate for the Calais commission, portrayed only the figure of Eustache de St. Pierre (see McNamara and Elsen 1977, p. 25).

## 18 JEAN D'AIRE, NUDE (REDUCTION)

Modeled 1885–1886, Musée Rodin cast 1976
Bronze
41 3/4 × 13 3/4 × 11 7/8 in. (106.1 × 34.9 × 30.2 cm)
Gift of the Iris and B. Gerald Cantor Foundation, 2009 (2009.1.19)

FIG. 18A: Auguste Rodin, *Study for Jean d'Aire* (detail), modeled 1884–1885, Musée Rodin cast 1971, bronze, H. 27 1/2 in., Iris and B. Gerald Cantor Center for Visual Arts at Stanford University, Gift of the Iris and B. Gerald Foundation, 1974.103.

After making the first maquette for *The Burghers of Calais* in 1884, Rodin created models of each of the individual figures for the second maquette specified by the Municipal Council of Calais. In the study of Jean d'Aire for the second maquette, completed the following year (FIG. 18A), the figure bears the keys to Calais on a cushion held between his hands; in the first maquette (CAT. 17), a single key was carried by Eustache de St. Pierre. Jean's feet are planted firmly on the ground, and his arms and torso are rigid—but his bald head is bowed as if he is still contemplating his decision. His robe hangs open, nearly falling off the right shoulder onto the ground. An air of defeat surrounds him, as if he is overcome by the dire fate he faces.

Rodin continued to work on the figure, making significant changes in Jean's demeanor even after the Municipal Council approved his second maquette for the commission. He modeled the figure in the nude as he did all the individual burghers, even though he knew in the final monument they would be wearing their sackcloth robes. He wished to use their entire bodies—their gait, carriage, and expression—to convey the inner turmoil each was undergoing as he considered the probable consequences of his patriotic self-sacrifice.

This is Rodin's final nude study for the figure of Jean d'Aire, and it is one of his most powerful and moving male nudes. Jean's face is careworn, his sunken cheeks and deep-set eye sockets indicating the physical toll the deprivations resulting from the siege of his city have exacted on his body. At the same time, Rodin uses his body to express the forcefulness of his determination. His muscles are tensed, his hands clenched into fists, outwardly expressing his internal battle to overcome his conflicting desires for self-sacrifice and self-preservation, as he heads out of the city to what he believes is his imminent death. The poet Rilke described Jean as a "man who would have lived for many years to come, but whose life is condensed into this sudden last hour, which he can hardly bear."[1] Yet Jean seems on the verge of overcoming his turmoil, facing his fate with determination, even defiance. By the end of 1888, Rodin had finished the final versions of the individual figures. Here Jean appears as he does in the final monument (FIG. 17), the most resolute of the six burghers. Head lifted, he looks straight ahead, his expression grim and noble. In the final monument, the graceful, downward flow of his robe enhances his uprightness and the dignity with which he advances to meet his death. His courage—and that of his companions—in the face of the harsh fate he believes awaits him would move his enemies to implore their king to spare the burghers' lives.

1 Elsen 1965, p. 138. Rilke continues, "His lips are tightly pressed together…There is fire in his strength, and it burns in his defiant bearing."

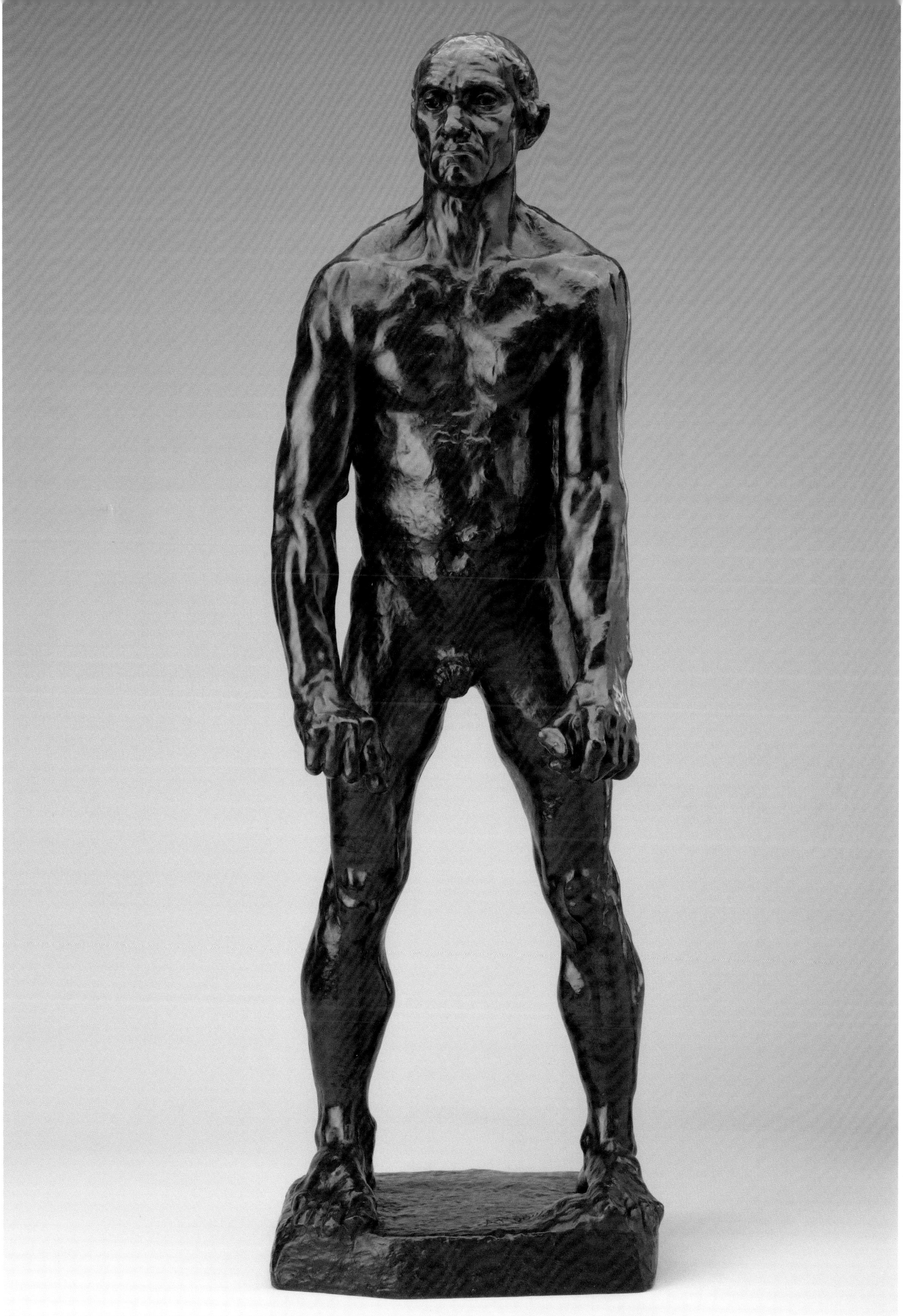

## 19 JEAN DE FIENNES, CLOTHED

Modeled 1885–1886, Musée Rodin cast 1983
Bronze
82 × 48 × 38 in. (208.3 × 121.9 × 96.5 cm)
Gift of the Iris and B. Gerald Cantor Foundation, 2009 (2009.1.20)

The original fourteenth-century account of the burghers of Calais mentions the names of only four of the six men who agreed to sacrifice themselves to save their fellow citizens. The name of Jean de Fiennes does not appear there; it was discovered in an account found in the Vatican Library in 1863, little more than twenty years before Rodin began work on the monument. Rodin decided to portray Jean as the youngest of the six burghers and realized the emotions Jean experienced would differ from those of his more mature peers. Jean's expression, hesitant pose, and awkward, open-handed gesture express the inner conflict the artist sought to portray. Jean has committed himself to the step he takes with his right foot, but his face betrays raw pain as he begins to turn and look back to the town, friends, and family members he may never see again, or perhaps, as Rilke says, back to himself (see quote). His feet push him onward, but he is not yet reconciled to the consequences of his decision. While his five comrades have at least acknowledged their fate, Jean has yet to come to terms with his.

*"The man moves forward, but he turns back once more, not to the city, not to those who are weeping, and not to those who go with him; he turns back on himself. His right arm is raised, bent, vacillating. His hands, open in the air as though to let something go, as one gives freedom to a bird. This gesture is symbolic of a departure from all uncertainty, from a happiness that has not yet been, from a grief that will now wait in vain, from men who live somewhere and whom he might have met sometime, from all possibilities of tomorrow and the day after tomorrow; and from death, which he had thought far distant, that he had imagined would come mildly and softly and at the end of a long, long time...*

*This figure, if placed by itself in a...garden, would be a monument for all who have died young."*

RAINER MARIA RILKE

Q Elsen 1965, pp. 138–39.

## 20 MONUMENTAL HEAD OF PIERRE DE WISSANT

Modeled circa 1884–1885, enlarged circa 1909, Musée Rodin cast 1980
Bronze
32 × 19 × 20 1/2 in. (81.3 × 48.3 × 52.1 cm)
Gift of the Iris and B. Gerald Cantor Foundation, 2009 (2009.1.21)

Rodin produced several models for the final, mournful head of Pierre de Wissant, whose features were modeled, ironically, on those of one of the comedian-actors in the Comédie Française. The artist used one of these models to create an independent sculpture that was ultimately cast in three sizes: small, life-size, and monumental. **In this much-larger-than-life version, what appears as tragic in the smaller versions becomes excruciating, amplifying Pierre's introspective agony to an almost unbearable intensity.** Every aspect of the emaciated burgher's features plays an expressive role. His head is turned slightly downward and to the right, as if he cannot bear the emotional pain his open mouth gives voice to.[1] His forehead is like a congealed lava flow, anguish piled upon anguish. A furrow between his brows plowed by Rodin's knuckles continues downward, denting the bridge of his nose. At the back of deeply hollowed sockets, his eyes are only partially molded, the lower portion excised or little more than a rough slash made in the clay model by Rodin's finger. The burgher's torn and battered lips, and even his eyebrows (no longer tufts of hair, but muscles contorted in pain), all serve to intensify his agony. The unconventional base of the sculpture elevates the head, emphasizing its isolation and fragmentary aspect, so the anguish becomes even more poignant. In the final model (FIG. 20A), Rodin used Pierre's entire body to express his pain and inner conflict; in this head these elements are so concentrated and intensified that they overwhelm the viewer.

FIG. 20A: Auguste Rodin, *Pierre de Wissant, Final Figure*, 1887, Musée Rodin cast 1981, bronze, 79 × 33 × 51 in., Iris and B. Gerald Cantor Center for Visual Arts at Stanford University, Gift of the B. Gerald Cantor Collection, 1992.148.

1 In the final model for the entire figure (FIG. 20A), Rodin used Pierre's outstretched neck to bend the head even farther downward as a counterpoint to his upraised right hand, emphasizing the emotional burden he bears.

## 21 ANDRIEU D'ANDRES

Modeled circa 1886–1887, Musée Rodin cast 1966
Bronze
18 1/2 × 7 1/4 × 8 1/2 in. (47 × 19.7 × 21.6 cm)
Gift of the Iris and B. Gerald Cantor Foundation, 2009 (2009.1.22)

In this reduced version of the final model for the figure of Andrieu d'Andres, Rodin captures the desperation of the burgher and his momentary ambivalence toward accepting his fate. "Another hides his head in his hands. After the heroic decision, after the superhuman act, [human] nature momentarily [reasserts] its rights, and this weakness of the flesh moves us to tears," was how one critic described the figure when a full-size plaster of the entire group was exhibited in the 1889 *Monet-Rodin* exhibition.[1]

FIG. 21A: Auguste Rodin, *Andrieu d'Andres, Second Maquette* (detail), 1885, Musée Rodin cast 1885, bronze, 23 1/4 × 18 5/8 × 9 in., Iris and B. Gerald Cantor Center for Visual Arts at Stanford University, Gift of the Iris and B. Gerald Cantor Foundation, 1974.101.

Rodin reworked the pose of the figure a number of times between the first maquette (CAT. 17) and this final model. Initially Andrieu's hands were placed on the side of his head. Rodin reworked the figure for the second maquette of 1885 (FIG. 21A), repositioning the hands so they overlapped at a right angle on top of the head. He also straightened the legs, moving the feet closer together and placing the figure on a downward slope, while maintaining the forward tilt of the upper body. These changes accentuated the physical—and emotional—instability of the figure.[2] By the following year he had completely changed the position of the legs, spreading them much farther apart and angling the feet to the figure's left. He also moved the hands more to the sides of the head so the fingers no longer overlap but interlock on top. The pose of the legs is somewhat similar to that which Rodin used for *Jean d'Aire* (CAT. 18), and it is worth noting Andrieu's features rather closely resemble Jean's.

In the final model, Rodin retained the pose of the hands but once again completely altered the pose of the left leg. Here the leg is bent sharply at the knee, at an angle that renders it incapable of providing support for the figure. The toes do not push the figure forward but barely touch the ground. The forward thrust of the figure that dominates the version modeled for the second maquette has been reduced considerably; anchored by the inward turn of the right foot, the figure no longer moves forward, halted by the fear and doubt that momentarily engulf him. The strong downward flow and deep folds of the drapery echo the pose of the head and arms, amplifying Andrieu's internal despair and emptiness.

1 Hugues Le Roux, "La vie à Paris," *Le Temps* (June 20, 1889), reprinted in Monet-Rodin 1889/1989, p. 219.

2 Nude and draped plasters of the life-size figure are shown in photographs of Rodin's studio at the time (see Elsen 2007, p. 123, FIGS. 95, 96).

## 22 CYBELE

Modeled circa 1889–1890, enlarged 1904–1905, Musée Rodin cast 1987
Bronze
65 × 34 × 56 in. (165.1 × 86.4 × 142.2 cm)
Gift of the Iris and B. Gerald Cantor Foundation, 2009 (2009.1.23)

In 1899 the smaller, original version of this work was shown in Amsterdam under the title *Abruzzezzi* (a reference to one of Rodin's favorite models, Anna Abruzzezzi (the sister of Adèle, who posed for *The Crouching Woman* [FIG. 10A]), marking one of the earliest occasions one of Rodin's partial figures was exhibited publicly. The following year it was displayed on a tall column with the title *Seated Woman*. The figure, a seated, headless woman with her right hand raised to her shoulder, relates closely to two other full-figure works exhibited about the same time, *Galatea* and *Shame* (also known as *Absolution*). A plaster model of the figure was enlarged to larger-than-life size in 1904 and exhibited at the 1905 Paris Salon as *Cybele*, along with a pendant figure of a reclining woman. Critical response was mixed. Some praised the "intensité de vie extraordinaire" that emanated from the two works.[1] One critic waxed enthusiastic about the figures' "sovereign amplitude, so moving, so connected by the palpitation of their forms to the universal life that [they] are the theology of sculpture."[2] Others, however, attacked Rodin for exhibiting "incomplete" and unfinished sculptures. One critic insisted *Cybele* needed to "return to the artist's studio and finish dressing; one doesn't present oneself in public while still a big fetus."[3] Holding to the traditional "academic" line of criticism, Adolphe Lambert wrote, "M. Rodin has exhibited ... two formless masses in plaster. When, then, will this powerfully talented artist understand that a sculptural work does not live by intentions, but by clear thought and precise forms, and that only that which is finished really matters!"[4]

The rough, unfinished surface of the work is amplified in the enlarged version. The hand and feet—parts of the figures usually given a great deal of attention by academic sculptors—are barely articulated here. The lumps and hollows of the flesh are greatly accentuated on this scale, so the body of the figure becomes a rocky landscape, a far cry from the usual smooth, perfect skin of the typical Salon goddess. Rodin made no attempt to cover the tool marks and mold joins that document the genesis of the figure.

It is worth noting the artist did not give the work its present name until 1914, more than twenty years after its creation, and then only after it had been enlarged, which more closely bound it to the scale and amplitude of an ancient cult statue. In ancient mythology Cybele was an "earth mother" goddess who ruled over all nature and saw to the fruitfulness of all creation. In antiquity she was typically identified by a number of attributes, including a sickle and a crown in the form of the turreted walls of a city (as she is represented in the NCMA's *The Triumph of Venice* [1737] by Pompeo Batoni), enthroned or riding in a chariot pulled by lions.

Rodin dispenses with these traditional iconographic attributes—and the head of the figure as well. Instead he employs the powerful, sensuous form of the body to convey the potent associations of fertility associated with the goddess. The truncation of the left arm—sliced at nearly the same angle as the neck—showcases the torsion of her body (especially apparent in profile) and accentuates the seated figure's upward thrust. The emphatic squaring off of the upper torso along the shoulders is a device Rodin used repeatedly, as in the figures of *Adam* (FIG. 4A), *The Three Shades* (CAT. 4), and *Meditation with Arms* (CAT. 25). The "incomplete" form reinforces the work's connections to classical sculpture. Reviewers compared it to *Venus de Milo*, *Victory of Samothrace*, and the pediment figures from the Parthenon, figures Rodin had studied during visits to the Louvre, the British Museum, and Italy.[5] However, the powerful torsion and exaggerated musculature (particularly noticeable on the figure's back) are the sculptor's own invention.

1 Eugène Morand, "Les Salons de 1905," *Gazette des beaux-arts*, 3e pér. 33 (1905), p. 484; Charles Morice in *Le Mercure de France* (June 1, 1905); and Louis Vauxcelles, "Sculpture," *Gil Blas* (April 14, 1905). These references (and those listed below) are cited in Lynne Ambrosini's fine entry in Ambrosini and Facos 1987, CAT. 49, pp. 149–55.

2 Maurice Hamel, *Les Arts* (May 24–25, 1905).

3 Auguste Daligny, *Le Journal des arts* (May 11, 1905).

4 *Triboulet* (April 30, 1905).

5 Louis Gillet, *Le Correspondant* (May 10, 1905); Louis Vauxcelles, op. cit.; A. Mockel, *L'Express* (April 21, 1905).

# BALZAC

FIG. 18: Louis-Auguste Bisson, *Honore de Balzac*, circa 1842.

FIG. 19: Auguste Rodin, *Dressing Gown Study for Balzac*, 1897, tissue coated with plaster, 58 1/4 × 22 1/2 × 16 1/2 in., Musée Rodin, Paris, S. 146.

FIG. 20: Auguste Rodin, *Balzac*, modeled 1891–1898, cast 1939, bronze, 111 × 48 1/4 × 41 in., Paris, Boulevard du Montparnasse.

A monument to Balzac (FIG. 20), author of a series of novels titled *The Human Comedy*, had been planned since the writer's death in 1850, but it was not until 1891 that, at the urging of their president, Émile Zola, the Société des Gens de Lettres de France offered the commission to Rodin. "I am happy to announce to you officially," he wrote, "that the Committee of the Société des Gens de Lettres, at their meeting of July 6th [1891], selected you by twelve votes against eight to execute the statue of Balzac, which is to be erected on the square of the Palais Royal... I shall feel personally obliged if you could push on your work as quickly as possible, and submit your plan in November. We all reckon on your great talent to give us a superb statue. Cordially yours, Émile Zola."[1]

Promising to deliver the final statue in January 1893, Rodin immersed himself in the study of Balzac, seeking to capture both the appearance and the soul of the man. He read and reread Balzac's literary works, pored over photographs and portraits, and visited the writer's birthplace of Tours to sketch its inhabitants. Rodin even hired Balzac's tailor to make a robe and a pair of trousers to the author's measurements so he could visualize his size and girth (FIG. 19).

Rodin perceived in Balzac a kindred spirit, and his quest to capture the essence of his subject became a seven-year obsession. He made more than fifty preliminary studies depicting the writer both nude and clothed, including *Nude Study of Balzac with Folded Arms ('C')* (CAT. 23) and *Nude Study of Balzac ('F' Athlete)* (CAT. 24). The 1893 deadline passed; then another, and another. Members of the Société sought to cancel the commission, and the affair erupted into a public scandal. But this paled in comparison to the shock, outrage, and ridicule that greeted the final model when it was finally exhibited to the public in May 1898. Critics described the statue as a "lump of plaster kicked together by a lunatic," "a sack of potatoes," "a pile of flour," "a snowman," and a "toad in a sack." The Société rejected the sculpture, and a wounded Rodin placed it in an open meadow near his home. "If truth is doomed to die," he said in a 1908 interview, "my *Balzac* will be cut into pieces by later generations. If truth is eternal, I predict that my statue will be its pathway. This work, which people laughed at, which they were careful to mock because they could not destroy it, is the product of my entire life, the mainspring of my aesthetic. From the day I created it, I was another man."[2] Twenty-two years after Rodin's death, the first bronze cast of the statue was erected in Paris in 1939 (FIG. 20). Today *Balzac* is regarded as one of the seminal works in the history of modern sculpture. Brancusi called it "the incontestable point of departure for modern sculpture."[3]

1 Lawton 1906, pp. 176–77.

2 Interview with a critic from *Le Matin* (July 13, 1908), in Cladel 1936, p. 223.

3 "Homage à Rodin," *Quatrième salon de la jeune sculptor*, exh. cat. (Paris, 1952), reprinted in Butler 1980, p. 150.

Q "Homage à Rodin," *Quatrième salon de la jeune sculptor*, exh. cat. (Paris, 1952), reprinted in Butler 1980, p. 150.

**FIG. 21:** Edward Steichen, *Toward the Light—Midnight, Balzac*, 1908, gum platinotype print, Musée Rodin, Paris, Ph. 226.

*"Since Michelangelo, sculptors wanted to make grandiose sculpture. They only succeeded in making grandiloquent sculpture... In the nineteenth century the position of sculpture was one of despair. Then Rodin arrived and transformed everything. Thanks to him, man once more became the measure, the model from which the statue rises. Thanks to him also sculpture became human again, both in its dimensions and in its spiritual content...The influence of Rodin was and remains immense...When he finished his Balzac, which remains the incontestable point of departure for modern sculpture, he declared, 'It is now that I would like to begin work.' The beautiful is absolute equity. Things are not difficult to make; what is difficult is putting ourselves in the state of mind to make them."*

CONSTANTIN BRANCUSI

## 23 NUDE STUDY OF BALZAC WITH FOLDED ARMS ('C')

Modeled 1892, Musée Rodin cast 1972
Bronze
30 × 16 3/4 × 13 1/2 in. (76.2 × 42.5 × 34.3 cm)
Gift of the Iris and B. Gerald Cantor Foundation, 2009 (2009.1.24)

This is one of numerous preliminary studies Rodin made for the Balzac commission.[1] He chose not to represent the writer as a young man, before he had produced the body of work that made him one of France's most celebrated authors, nor in his later years when he had become debauched and grossly fat. Here he portrays Balzac in middle age, somewhat past his physical prime, but with strong legs—much longer proportionally than Balzac's own—defiantly crossed arms, square shoulders, ample body, and penetrating gaze all conveying an attitude of confidence and no-nonsense physicality. In spite of Rodin's efforts to present an accurate physical image of the writer, and to capture Balzac's restless creative mind ("I shall carry a world in my head," Balzac proclaimed), the committee was dismayed by Rodin's model. According to one account, when the committee visited Rodin's studio to see a large (fifty-inch) version of the study in 1892, one of them exclaimed, "Well, well, you are making a buffoon [*triboulet*]." The account continues, "After having studied his subject, the drawings of him, and his books and even his own homeland, the artist had conceived of a strange Balzac, in the attitude of a wrestler, seeming to defy the world. He had put over very widely spread legs an enormous belly. More concerned with an exact resemblance than with the usual conception of Balzac, he made him shocking, deformed, his head sunk into his shoulder. The [committee members] were all the more disappointed since they were counting on Rodin. Nevertheless, with the greatest respect they explained to him that he had the obligation to represent Balzac at an age when he was less portly and when his neck had not disappeared beneath layers of fat."[2]

Other writers were more sympathetic. His biographer Judith Cladel noted the figure's assertive stance was that of a warrior marching into battle.[3] The latter comment reflects Rodin's own aims. In 1894 he wrote to Jean Aicard, who had succeeded Zola as president of the Society: "I ask that you provide me the means to honor, with all my might, with all my will, the great man... I think of [Balzac's] relentless labor, of the difficulties of his life, of his incessant battles and of his great courage. I wish to express all that."[4] Rodin seems to have held this particular representation of Balzac in high regard, since he had a reduced version made, from which the present work was cast.

*In 1894 the writer Séverine (whom Rodin described as "the angel of eloquence") described what was probably the larger version of* Nude Study of Balzac with Folded Arms, *which she had seen in Rodin's studio: "He was very ugly, the skin as if flayed, the face barely indicated... But from that formless face, with deep sockets, with a grin like a scar... with the jawbone of a cannibal, with a rugged forehead embossed beneath a mass of hair like a clump of weeds, there emanated such an imperious sovereignty, almost superhuman."*

1 It seems likely the massive, somewhat ungainly, supporting wedge between the legs, particularly the way it is connected to the left leg, would have been reduced in mass or eliminated, even if the figure was to be draped in the final monument.

2 Charles Chincholle, "Le *Balzac* et Rodin," *Le Figaro*, 329 (November 25, 1894), p. 3.

3 Cladel 1936, p. 189.

4 Cladel 1936, p. 194.

Q Séverine, "Les dix mille francs de Rodin," *Le Journal* (Paris, November 27, 1894), in Tancock 1976, pp. 434, 448, n. 30.

## 24 NUDE STUDY OF BALZAC ('F' ATHLETE)

Modeled 1896, Musée Rodin cast 1974
Bronze
37 × 16 × 15 1/2 in. (94 × 40.6 × 39.4 cm)
Gift of the Iris and B. Gerald Cantor Foundation, 2009 (2009.1.25)

This is probably one of the final nude studies Rodin modeled for the figure concealed beneath the long robe in the final version of the Balzac monument. Here, perhaps in response to the commission's criticism of his earlier study (CAT. 23), Rodin presents a young, virile, athletic figure whose musculature has been given greater emphasis, particularly in the forearms, back, and legs. **Knowing that the body would be hidden beneath a voluminous dressing gown in the final statue, Rodin seems to have used this as a working model.** Sections of flesh appear to have been cut away from the plaster model at the top of the torso and along the spine. The figure is dotted with an array of odd knobs, lumps, and ridges, which Elsen hypothesized may have been added to facilitate the draping of the figure for the final version.[1] Visible across the back and legs is the imprint of the texture of the coarse damp cloths Rodin used to keep the original model moist as he worked on it over time.

Most surprising—even shocking—was Rodin's decision to position the model's hands crossed over his groin, one hand grasping his erect penis. It is possible this pose would have lent bulk to the writer's body under his robe, but it is a stretch to imagine Rodin's decision was merely a technical means to a formal end. Was Rodin, who had spent years researching the writer's personality and lifestyle, connecting Balzac's consuming sexuality with his creative genius, articulating, as one writer suggested, "a more complex, synthetic attitude towards Balzac's character, one that associates cerebration with procreation"?[2] Was he referring to the author's well-known erotic predilections? Was Rodin, a creative genius of similar consuming sexuality, making a more personal statement?[3] Or, aware as he was of the negative opinions expressed about his statue, and knowing the gesture would be concealed beneath the robe in the final version, could it be the artist was also taking a private jab at his critics?

1 Elsen 2003, p. 405.

2 Michelle Facos, in Ambrosini and Facos 1987, p. 130. Balzac himself identified artistic creativity with sexual prowess, explaining in a letter to his future wife, the Countess Eveline Hanska, that he prepared himself to write his novels by "masturbating his brain" (see Elsen 2003, pp. 375–76, 390, n. 71).

3 Cf. Rodin's *The Sculptor and His Muse*, where the Muse is represented in the act of sexually stimulating the sculptor (a brief but interesting discussion on the issue of sex and creativity in the context of this work is found in De Caso and Sanders 1977, pp. 49–53).

## 25 MEDITATION WITH ARMS

Modeled after 1900, Musée Rodin cast 1980
Bronze
61 × 25 × 25 in. (154.9 × 63.5 × 63.5 cm)
Gift of the Iris and B. Gerald Cantor Foundation, 2009 (2009.1.26)

FIG. 25A: Auguste Rodin, *Meditation without Arms*, 1894–1896, Musée Rodin cast 1981, bronze, 57 1/2 × 28 × 22 1/8 in., Iris and B. Gerald Cantor Center for Visual Arts at Stanford University, Gift of the B. Gerald Cantor Collection, 1992.136.

Rodin originally conceived of this figure without arms and exhibited a large version in this form in 1897. In discussing this piece, one of the studies related to Rodin's *Monument to Victor Hugo*, Rilke noted, "It is striking that the arms are lacking. Rodin must have considered these arms as too facile a solution of his task, as something that did not belong to that body which desired to envelop itself without any external aid ... The same completeness is conveyed in all the armless statues of Rodin; nothing vital is missing. One stands before them as if before a completed whole that brooks no complement."[1]

Sometime after 1900 Rodin decided to add the massive arms, deliberately leaving visible the joins required to accomplish the additions. In fact many joins, casting seams, and patches are evident throughout the figure, as if the artist wished to emphasize the manner in which the figure was "manufactured." The figure is an amalgam of masculine and feminine parts. The massive legs and arms, the squared-off upper contours of the shoulders, the unnatural stretch of the neck, and the position of the head all have their origins in Rodin's *Adam* (FIG. 4A). Almost hidden within the encircling arms is the beautiful feminine head, turned downward and inward like that of *Fallen Caryatid with a Stone* (CAT. 7). The anatomy of the figure and the articulation of the bones and muscles have been distorted, as, for example, the alignment of the spine with the lower half of the body and the chest to the lower torso, the overlarge feet, and the awkward join of the left foot to the lower leg. Analyzed anatomically, the sway and inward bending of the torso seem highly improbable and unnatural, yet they enhance the torsion of the figure. Rodin himself offered this insight: "The artist ... exaggerates or deforms the literal in sculpture ... He suppresses or diminishes one part; and yet the whole is true because he seeks only truth."[2]

Rodin's search for truth in the *Meditation* figures led him to deliberately turn away from long-established canons of ideal beauty and pursue his own vision. Elsen noted, "Rodin was the first sculptor to see the body abstractly, *and to act accordingly on his sculptures*. Thus artistic form won over anatomical form."[3] Rodin understood the body, in all its varied forms and poses, as a vessel that contained and reflected inner beauty.

*"Again and again in his figures Rodin returned to this bending inward, to this intense listening to one's own depth. This is seen in the wonderful figure called 'La Méditation'... Never before was a human body assembled to such an extent about its inner self, so bent by its own soul and yet upheld by the elastic strength of its blood. The neck, bent sidewise on the lowered body, rises and stretches and holds the listening head over the distant roar of life."*

RAINER MARIA RILKE

1 Elsen 1965, p. 123.

2 Lawton 1906, p. 161.

3 Elsen 2003, p. 243.

Q Elsen 1965, pp. 122–23.

## 26 NAKED MUSE, WITHOUT ARMS (STUDY FOR "THE MONUMENT TO WHISTLER")

Modeled 1905–1906, enlarged 1907–1908, Musée Rodin cast 1991
Bronze
88 × 35 1/2 × 42 7/8 in. (223.5 × 90.2 × 108.9 cm)
Gift of the Iris and B. Gerald Cantor Foundation, 2010 (2010.1)

In December 1903 Rodin was elected president of the International Society of Sculptors, Painters, and Gravers, succeeding James McNeill Whistler, who had served as its first president. At a May 1905 meeting of the membership, it was suggested Rodin be invited "to make some monument to Whistler." The suggested theme of the monument was to be "Winged Victory symbolizing Whistler's triumph—the triumph of Art over the Enemies."[1] Rodin agreed to take on the commission for the cost of his expenses only. A public subscription was launched and quickly raised the funds to underwrite the monument, which was to be installed on the Chelsea Embankment in London, and a replica cast for the grounds outside Whistler's birthplace in Lowell, Massachusetts. In spite of this auspicious start, the monument was never completed.

Rodin's initial sketches for the monument show that his first idea was to represent a winged figure draping a garland over a medallion bearing a relief portrait of Whistler. The model—and probably the inspirational muse—for the figure was Gwen John, who entered Rodin's life in 1904–5, when she came to his studio seeking work as a model. She was twenty-seven and the artist was sixty-three. She fell passionately in love with Rodin and soon became his lover. Their affair intensified during the period Rodin was most actively working on the Whistler project. Over the course of the next few years, Rodin's conception of the monument evolved, undoubtedly colored by the relationship. The Victory figure was transformed into a muse ascending a mount and became the sole figurative element of the work, Rodin having decided to eliminate the portrait of Whistler.

By 1907–8 the figure appeared much as it looks here: nude, without arms, head downturned, with the left foot supported somewhat awkwardly on a rocky plinth upon which the figure rests. An enlarged plaster, of similar dimensions to the present work, was exhibited at the Salon of 1908 under the title *The Muse: Climbing the Mountain of Fame*. There it was generally scorned by critics, the most savage of whom was André Beaunier in the *Gazette des beaux-arts*: "Imagine a woman, a sort of woman, standing, the left leg raised, leaning on some rock; and this woman looks at her left foot; she would look at it, at least, if she had eyes. Why she shows interest in this inferior member one doesn't know...The neck is an absurd cylinder. The head is that of a brute...Rodin never ends by completing an ensemble."[2] The artist's ardent supporter Gustave Geffroy was far more positive in his assessment. Perhaps thinking of the Louvre's ancient, armless masterpiece *Venus de Milo*, Geffroy also drew attention to the fragmentary aspect of the figure: "The result here is equal to the works of Greece; there is the same plenitude, the same vital force of the modeling. I understand how people might regret the lack of arms. It is understandable and I would like to regret them also. But before regretting what isn't there, permit us to admire what is there: a masterpiece, a great masterpiece."[3]

Rodin continued to work on the sculpture, experimenting with different plaster-soaked linen cloths to drape the lower half of the figure (which would have further enhanced the similarity of its appearance to that of *Venus de Milo*). In 1909 he sent a photograph of the armless draped figure to the Whistler committee. Soon afterward Rodin's progress on the monument seems to have ground to a standstill, although it continued to occupy a prominent place in his studio. Once he added drapery to the lower half of the figure, it must have seemed complete to him; additions like the arms or the portrait medallion might have seemed extraneous. Another factor in his unwillingness to continue any sustained work on the monument may have been more personal: his complicated feelings for Gwen John, who continued to be devoted to Rodin well after their relationship ended.

Rodin's lack of progress on the piece must have frustrated the committee (whose sentiments undoubtedly echoed those of earlier committees who had experienced similar struggles with the artist on previous monumental commissions like *Victor Hugo* and *Balzac*). Rodin attempted to publicly defend himself when he spoke to a reporter from the *Morning Post* of London: "It is impossible for me to fix a time for the completion of a work of art. I am unfortunately a slow worker, being one of those artists in whose minds the conception of work slowly

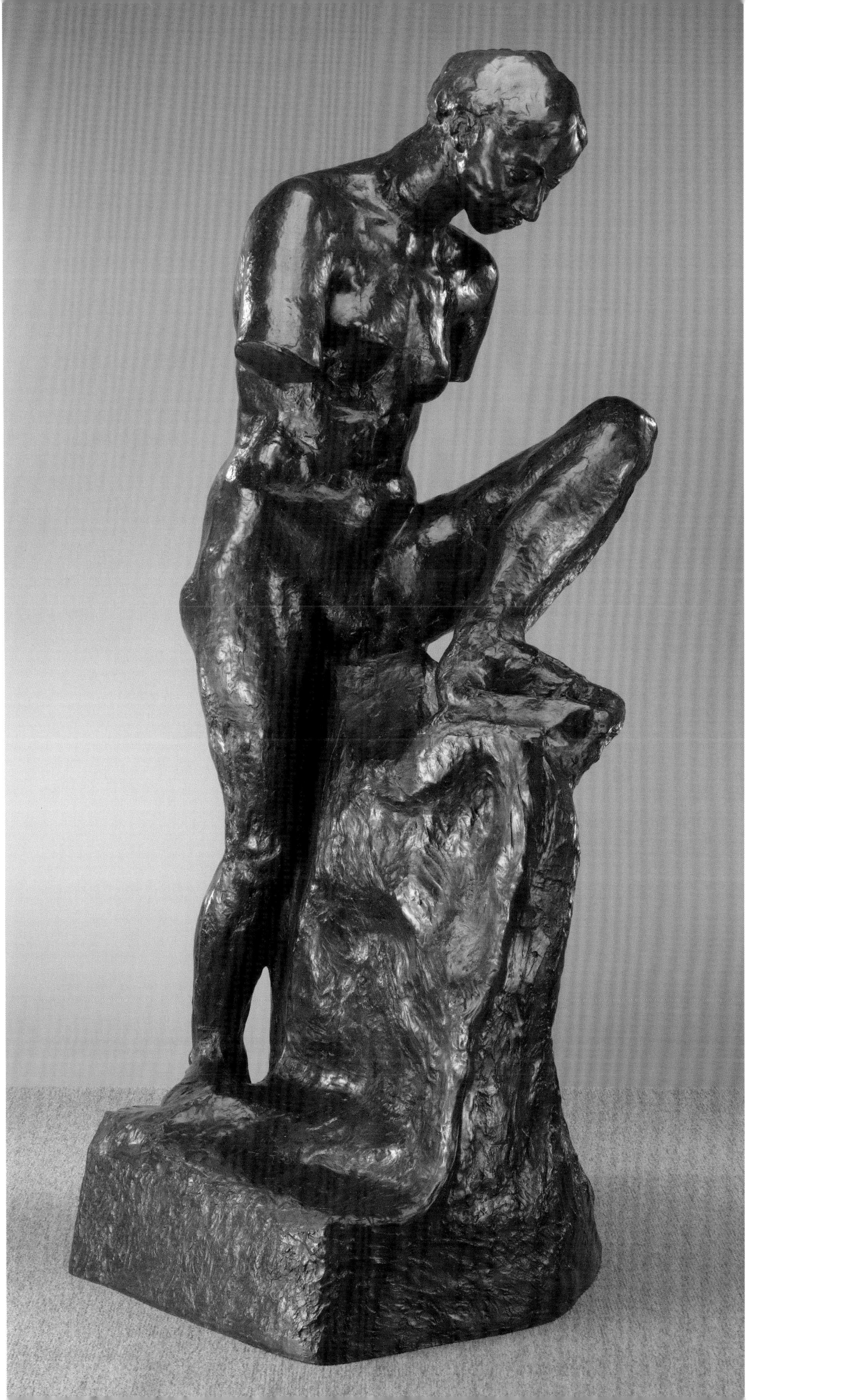

takes shape & slowly comes to maturity. I lay my work aside while it is yet unfinished, & for months I may appear to abandon it. Every now & then, however, I return to it & correct it or add a detail here & there. I have not really abandoned it, you see, only I am hard to satisfy."[4]

Rodin communicated sporadically with the committee over the next few years, writing in November 1913 that the statue was nearing completion, and again in April 1916 that he would be unable to have it cast in bronze until after the war ended, because all supplies of bronze were needed for the war effort. By this time the artist's health was declining, and it appears he worked no further on the monument to Whistler.

Finally in April 1919, more than a year after Rodin's death, committee members traveled to Paris to appraise what they had been informed by Léonce Bénédite, the first curator of the Musée Rodin, was the final maquette for the monument. It appears likely Bénédite, who had complete access to Rodin's studio after the artist's death, made several clumsy additions to the model, including the very awkward right arm and overlarge hand; a nonsensical, decorative skin of drapery and garlands trailing down the surface of the rocky "mount"; and a crude likeness of Whistler on a medallion at the base (FIG. 26A). The committee's verdict was highly critical: "The statue, in its incomplete state, is in no way worthy to commemorate the genius of Whistler, and is not a work that Rodin himself would have presented to the public."[5] The committee refused to accept the work or pay for it and demanded the return of funds they had committed toward the monument.

FIG. 26A: The model for *The Monument to Whistler*, sculpture completed after Rodin's death, Pennell Archives, Library of Congress, Washington, D.C., inv. no. 93506142.

1 Newton and MacDonald 1978, p. 221. This article remains the most thorough study on the commission.

2 *Gazette des beaux-arts* 39 (January–June 1908), in Newton and MacDonald 1978, p. 224.

3 "Les salons de 1908," *La Dépéche [de Toulouse]*, no. 14533 (April 20, 1908), p. 1.

4 February 15, 1910, in Newton and MacDonald 1978, p. 226.

5 Letter from the committee's chairman to Bénédite, May 8, 1919, in Newton and MacDonald 1978, p. 231.

"The result here is equal to the works of Greece; there is the same plenitude, the same vital force of the modeling. I understand how people might regret the lack of arms. It is understandable and I would like to regret them also. But before regretting what isn't there, permit us to admire what is there: a masterpiece, a great masterpiece."

# 27 MONUMENTAL TORSO OF THE WALKING MAN

Modeled circa 1906, Musée Rodin cast 1985
Bronze
43 1/2 × 26 3/4 × 15 in. (110.1 × 67.9 × 38.1 cm)
Gift of the Iris and B. Gerald Cantor Foundation, 2009 (2009.1.4)

FIG. 27A: Auguste Rodin, *The Walking Man*, 1876 and 1899 or 1900, Musée Rodin cast 1970, bronze with black and green patina, 33 × 20 1/4 × 20 in., Iris and B. Gerald Cantor Center for Visual Arts at Stanford University, Gift of B. Gerald Cantor, 1982.306.

FIG: 27B: Roman, *Torso of an Emperor in the Guise of Jupiter*, 1st century, marble, 56 1/2 × 29 1/2 × 15 1/2 in., North Carolina Museum of Art, Raleigh, Gift of Mr. and Mrs. Gordon Hanes.

Rodin typically conceived his figures first in terms of their torsos, subsequently adding, when he felt the need, arms, legs, and heads. This powerful torso had its origins in the preliminary studies Rodin modeled about 1880 for his *St. John the Baptist Preaching* (CAT. 3), when the influence of Michelangelo's works, which he had studied during his 1876 trip to Italy, was still strong. In the only letter that survives from this trip, Rodin wrote to his future wife, Rose Beuret, "Let me tell you, since my first hour in Florence I have been making a study of Michelangelo; that will not astonish you, and I believe the great magician is giving up a few of his secrets to me."[1] The piece also betrays Rodin's careful study of classical sculpture (FIG. 27B).

One of these torso studies, somewhat battered, remained in Rodin's studio for nearly twenty years. Sometime around 1899–1900, the artist rediscovered the torso, which included a portion of the right thigh, and he exhibited casts of it as an independent work before joining it to a pair of legs he had likewise modeled as a study for *St. John*. Thus was born *The Walking Man* (FIG. 27A). The present work derived directly from this model; all Rodin seems to have done is amputate the extended portion of the right leg and add a crude base upon which the torso rests. Rodin ordered an enlarged plaster version, which more approximated the size of the monumental ancient fragments he had studied in Rome and at the Louvre. Bronze versions in this size were cast by the Musée Rodin in 1985–86.

What is most astonishing about this piece is the amount of violence—both accidental and deliberate—it seems to have undergone. Large chunks of material have been gouged out from under the front of both shoulders. On the figure's right side, the gouged-out area is left rough, as if stone had crumbled away from a marble, while the other side looks as if the piece had been cut away with a blade. Horizontal gashes have been opened across the upper and lower abdomen, as if it had been slashed by a sword. The back of the figure is even rougher in appearance. Rodin kept numerous seams visible, deliberately leaving evidence of the piece's manufacture. Most noticeable of all is a deep depression—a hole, really—where it appears the artist stuck his hand into the wet clay model and clawed out a large chunk (see back cover). In late works such as this, *Cybele* (CAT. 22) and *Naked Muse, without Arms (study for "The Monument to Whistler")* (CAT. 26), **Rodin rejected both classical and traditional academic ideals to create works in which the intensely worked surface becomes a means for expression.**

1 Rodin 1985, p. 34, n. 13.

## 28 THE CATHEDRAL

Modeled 1908, Musée Rodin cast 1955
Bronze
25 1/4 × 12 3/4 × 13 1/2 in. (64.1 × 32.3 × 34.3 cm)
Gift of the Iris and B. Gerald Cantor Foundation, 2009 (2009.1.27)

Rodin was fascinated with the diverse forms of hands, and he modeled many of them in rapid clay sketches. He kept dozens of these models in his studio as a kind of repertoire, attaching different hands at varying angles to his figures to explore the expressive possibilities that each combination might reveal. Several of these hands were subsequently cast in bronze as independent works of art, occasionally in combination with other figures or partial figures (for example, *Large Clenched Hand with Imploring Figure* and *Hand of Rodin Holding a Torso*). This working method encouraged Rodin's interest in the fragment—and inspired the radical concept that individual forms like hands are not necessarily dependent upon a larger whole to convey meaning. As early as 1900, he was hailed as "the sculptor of hands, of furious, clenched, reared-up, damned hands ... hands that writhe as though to grasp the void ... sad hands, furious and tired, full of energy... hands of one who has embraced chimeras or passions, hands of heroism or hands of vice."[1]

Rodin created *Cathedral* by using two separate plaster hands, which he joined together at their bases. A wedge of plaster was inserted to fill in the gap between the two plasters and was rather cursorily covered over before the piece was cast in bronze.[2]

It is a measure of Rodin's genius that he could use a motif as mundane as a hand to create a work of art as evocative as *The Cathedral*. The arched hands bring to mind the vault of a Gothic cathedral and can be seen as an outgrowth of Rodin's interest in medieval architecture, which culminated in the publication of his *Cathedrals of France* in 1914. The sculpture was given its present title only after Rodin's book was published. The sculpture had originally been given the evocative title *The Ark of the Covenant*, suggesting the space itself was a repository of mystical, divine power. The sculpture is closely related to Rodin's study for another work, *The Secret*, where a casket is held between the two hands. Here the fingers of the two hands lightly touch, as if about to be joined in prayer, but the space between them remains empty, mysterious, and evocative. Given the intimacy of this gesture, it comes as a surprise that Rodin has used two nearly identical right hands.[3] Thus notes critic Leo Steinberg, they are "forever caught in marveling reciprocal self-contemplation."[4]

1 Gustave Kahn, "Les Mains chez Rodin," *Rodin et son oeuvre, La Plume* (Paris, 1900), pp. 12–13; also see Rilke, in Elsen 1965, pp. 123–24.

2 This is evident upon close examination of the base, particularly on the side where the signature appears.

3 As Le Normand-Romain noted (2007, I, p. 252), one writer saw Rodin's use of two nearly identical hands as evidence of his hasty working method and his random use of bozzetti, while another argued strongly that the hands belonged to different people.

4 Steinberg 1972, p. 358.

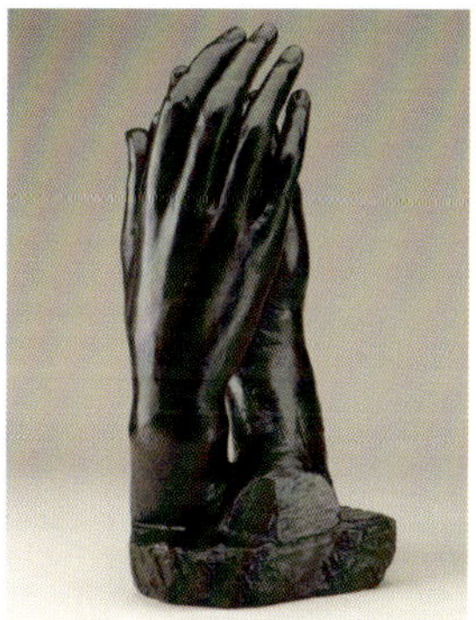

## 29 THE PRAYER

Modeled 1910, Musée Rodin cast 1979
Bronze
49 1/2 × 21 5/8 × 19 5/8 in. (125.7 × 54.9 × 49.8 cm)
Gift of the Iris and B. Gerald Cantor Foundation, 2009 (2009.1.28)

*The Prayer* is one of the many works that issued from *The Gates of Hell*. In the upper right corner of the tympanum is a horizontal female figure whose hands are clasped over her abdomen (FIG. 29A). Rodin removed the head and arms from one of the plaster models of this work, and after further experimentation (combining it with another female nude, removing the right leg completely), he added a base to the truncated legs and exhibited the piece in a vertical position. In 1900 and 1902, a cast was exhibited (as *Kneeling Figure*) atop a column adorned with hearts.

The model was enlarged before 1908, when it was illustrated in a biography of Rodin under the title *The Prayer*, probably because the figure's partial legs suggested it was kneeling, and the angle at which the neck was cut hinted at the downward tilt of an absent head. The sensuous form of the kneeling female figure also held a spiritual significance for the artist. As Rodin observed in his *Cathedrals of France*, "Woman is the true Holy Grail, never more beautiful than when kneeling. The Gothics knew this. The church from the outside is shaped like a woman on her knees."[1]

*The Prayer* reflects Rodin's pursuit of his belief that a partial figure was a complete work of art, since it could completely express the artist's intent. As Elsen noted, *The Prayer* deserves "the designation *sculpture* rather than *statue*."[2] After 1900 Rodin repeatedly exhibited these "incomplete" forms, to the bewilderment and consternation of the public and many critics alike. When a plaster version of *The Prayer* was shown at the Salon of 1910 (as a pendant to *Torso of a Young Woman*), one reviewer wrote: "[We] regret that such a vanquisher of material confines himself to his *études*, that such a modeler of flesh has put so much perseverance into a sketch. Virginal or powerful, each of these two feminine torsos is a palpitating fragment of a goddess."[3] Another reviewer was far less charitable: "What we discover first...are a number of projects for ruins: women cut up in pieces, torsos without heads, legs and arms, chests without backs, backs without chests—a foot. All of which are signed by the names of the most official and most venerable masters, such as M. Rodin, and perched in places of honor and in the best possible light."[4] *The Prayer* and a sculpture by Rodin's one-time pupil Bourdelle were caricatured in a cartoon published in the *Paris-Journal* in 1910, which showed Bourdelle's *Hercules the Archer* surrounded by a crowd of awestruck women and an equally admiring group of men surrounding *The Prayer*. The cartoon bore the caption: "Female choir: 'Ah! A whole man! What a dream! Bravo Bourdelle!' Male choir: 'Ah! A headless woman! What a dream! Bravo Rodin.'"[5]

Although Rodin's insistent view that the partial figure was a true work of art and that beauty could be expressed in a fragment shocked traditionalists, it was a revelation to more forward-looking individuals, particularly artists of the next generation. In distilling the human figure to its purest, most basic form, Rodin opened the way for other early-twentieth-century sculptors such as Maillol, Lachaise, and Lehmbruck.

FIG. 29A: Auguste Rodin, *The Prayer*, detail from *The Gates of Hell*, 1880–1900, Musée Rodin cast 1981, bronze, Iris and B. Gerald Cantor Center for Visual Arts, Stanford University, Gift of B. Gerald Cantor Collection, 1985.86.

1 Rodin 1914, p. 29.

2 Elsen 2003, p. 278.

3 Raymond Bouyer, "Les salons de 1910: La sculpture," *La revue de l'art*, 159 (June 1910), p. 428.

4 *La Sizeranne* (Paris, June 1910), in Le Normand-Romain 2007, II, p. 617.

5 Illustrated in Le Normand-Romain 2007, II, p. 617.

**Camille Claudel**
French, 1864–1943

## 30 BUST OF RODIN

Modeled 1888–1892, date of cast unknown
Bronze
15 3/4 × 9 1/4 × 11 in. (40 × 23.5 × 28 cm)
Gift of the Iris and B. Gerald Cantor Foundation, 2009 (2009.1.29)

Rodin met the seventeen-year-old Camille Claudel in 1882 while supervising a small group of young women artists as a favor to his friend, the sculptor Alfred Boucher, who was departing Paris to study in Rome. Shortly thereafter Rodin sculpted his first portrait of her, *Camille Claudel with Short Hair*.[1] In 1884 she entered Rodin's atelier as a student and soon became his assistant. By this time Rodin was clearly smitten with her; he addresses a letter to her "ma féroce amie," and his sculptures *Eternal Springtime* and *Thought* (FIG. 30A), which reflect his passion for her, date from 1884 to 1885.[2] In addition to her roles as Rodin's mistress and muse, Camille became his collaborator (his "perceptive and sagacious coworker" is how one writer described her role during this period), modeling the hands and feet of many of his works, including some of *The Burghers of Calais*.[3] Her face and body pervade Rodin's works of the 1880s and early 1890s, and their passionate, tormented relationship inspired several works Rodin created during this period.

During this time Camille pursued her own career. Her works from this period are quite close to Rodin's, as both artists were drawing inspiration from similar sources, above all each other. The relationship ended in 1892, at least in part because Camille was unwilling to accept Rodin's continuing relationship with Rose Beuret. Rodin was distraught at their separation; Camille never recovered. She became obsessed with the idea that Rodin had sapped her artistic energies, had fed on her genius. Her psychosis became increasingly acute, and in 1913 she was confined to an asylum, where she remained for the last thirty years of her life.

Although Rodin sculpted Camille's features many times over the course of their relationship, this is the only sculpture she made of him. Claudel began work on this portrait at the height of their affair. Sculpted in a style similar to Rodin's, the work joins the head to the mass of the base through the sculptor's flowing beard. Although the work was modeled in clay, the blocklike mass of Rodin's head (best seen in profile), appears to have been chiseled from a block of stone, then modeled by Camille's fingers.[4] The lower half of the bust is dominated by Rodin's beard—not so much a beard as a craggy landscape excavated by Camille's fingers and thumb. The mouth remains hidden, as if she could not decide on what expression best suited her lover, or perhaps she wished to let Rodin's eyes and furrowed brow express his forceful personality and intelligence.

Camille exhibited the bust in 1892, and the following year the eminent critic Octave Mirbeau hailed it as "a marvel of powerful interpretation, of verve, of great bearing."[5] A few years later Matthias Morhardt would describe it as "a severe work…patient and reflective; each detail representing a new sort of testimony…in short it is a dramatic work; she presents him majestically as a granite-like construction of old age."[6] Camille's brother, Paul, described this work as "a true architectural realization of the human animal, the animation of the bones that make the flesh function, that awakens a face. He is here with his own look. But it was not just his face that made sense for her."[7] Rodin himself greatly admired this sculpture, pronouncing it his favorite likeness of himself. He had it cast in bronze at his own expense, and when it was exhibited at the Salon of 1892, he twice requested it be moved to a more favorable location.

FIG. 30A (LEFT): Auguste Rodin, *Thought*, 1893–1895, marble, H. 29 1/8 in., Musée Rodin, Paris, S. 1003.

1 Le Normand-Romain 2007, I, pp. 265–67.

2 The entire letter is reproduced in Paris and La Chapelle 1990, pp. 19–20 (excerpts are translated in Butler 1993, p. 184). An even more surprising indication of the depths of Rodin's passion is evidenced by the "contract" he wrote (the terms must have been Camille's) on October 12, 1886 (reproduced in Paris and La Chapelle, pp. 20–21; translated in Butler, p. 198). The best discussion in English of Rodin's relationship with Camille is Antoinette Le Normand-Romain, *Camille Claudel and Rodin: Time Will Heal Everything* (Paris: Editions du Musée Rodin, 2003) (also see Butler, pp. 180–98, 268–84). A harsher view of Camille and her relationship with Rodin appears in J. Adolf Schmoll Eisenwerth, *Auguste Rodin and Camille Claudel*, trans. John Omrod (New York: Prestel, 1999).

3 Morhardt 1898, pp. 718–19.

4 In a letter to his wife dated September 2, 1902, Rilke described his initial impression of Rodin: "The forehead, the way it stands in relation to the nose, which goes out from it like a ship leaving the harbor—is very remarkable. There is something sculptural in this brow and nose" (reprinted and translated in Butler 1980, p. 113).

5 "Le Salon de 1893," *La Revue encyclopédique Larousse*, in Paris and La Chapelle 1990, p. 123.

6 Morhardt 1898, p. 730.

7 Preface to the catalogue of the exhibition *Camille Claudel* (Paris: Musée Rodin, 1951), p. 11.

# SELECTED BIBLIOGRAPHY

Alexandre 1900. Alexandre, Arsène. *Exposition de 1900: L'Oeuvre de Rodin.* Paris: Société d'édition artistique, 1900.

Alexandre 1909. Alexandre, Arsène. "Auguste Rodin—Le Penseur." *Chroniques d'Art.* Paris, May 1909.

Ambrosini and Facos 1987. Ambrosini, Lynne, and Facos, Michelle. *Rodin: The Cantor Gift to the Brooklyn Museum.* New York: Brooklyn Museum, 1987.

Bartlett 1889. Bartlett, Truman H. "Auguste Rodin, Sculptor." Originally published in *The American Architect and Building News.* Boston, XXV, 1889. Reprinted in Elsen 1965, pp. 13–109.

Baudelaire 1846. Baudelaire, Charles. *Le Salon de 1846,* XVI. "Pourquoi la sculpture est ennuyeuse," XVIII. "De L'Héroïsme de la vie moderne." Ed. cit., Kelley 1975.

Beausire 1988. Beausire, Alain. *Quand Rodin exposait.* Paris: Musée Rodin, 1988.

Bordeaux 1975. Bordeaux, Jean-Luc. "Some Reflections on Rodin's *The Kiss. Gazette des beaux-arts* 86, no. 117 (October 1975), pp. 123–28.

Butler 1980. Butler, Ruth, ed. *Rodin in Perspective.* Englewood Cliffs, N.J.: Prentice-Hall, 1980.

Butler 1993. Butler, Ruth. *Rodin: The Shape of Genius.* New Haven: Yale University Press, 1993.

Cladel 1917. Cladel, Judith. *Rodin, the Man and His Art with Leaves from His Notebook.* Trans. S. K. Star. New York: Century, 1917.

Cladel 1936. Cladel, Judith. *Rodin, sa vie glorieuse, sa vie inconnue.* Paris: Bernard Grasset, 1936.

Coquiot 1917. Coquiot, Gustave. *Rodin à l'hôtel de Biron et à Meudon.* Paris: Librairie Ollendorff, 1917.

Dante 1975. Alighieri, Dante. *La Commedia secondo l'antico vulgate.* Ed. Giorgio Petrocchi. Turin: Einaudi, 1975.

Dante 1995. *The Divine Comedy.* Trans. Allen Mandelbaum. New York: Alfred Knopf, 1995.

De Caso and Sanders 1977. De Caso, Jacques, and Sanders, Patricia. *Rodin's Sculpture: A Critical Study of the Spreckels Collection, California Palace of the Legion of Honor.* San Francisco: Fine Arts Museums of San Francisco, 1977.

Dujardin-Beaumetz 1913. Dujardin-Beaumetz, Henri Charles Etienne. *Entretiens avec Rodin.* Paris: Imprimerie Paul Dupont, 1913. Ed. cit. Paris: Musée Rodin, 1992. Trans. and reprinted in Elsen 1965, pp. 145–85.

Elsen 1960. Elsen, Albert E. *Rodin's* The Gates of Hell. Minneapolis: University of Minnesota Press, 1960.

Elsen 1963. Elsen, Albert E. *Rodin.* Exh. cat. New York: Museum of Modern Art, 1963.

Elsen 1965. Elsen, Albert E., ed. *Auguste Rodin: Readings on His Life and Work.* Englewood Cliffs, N.J.: Prentice-Hall, 1965.

Elsen 1967. Elsen, Albert E. "Rodin's Naked *Balzac.*" *Burlington Magazine* 109 (November 1967), pp. 606–17.

Elsen 1985a. Elsen, Albert E. "The Gates of Hell" *by Auguste Rodin.* Stanford: Stanford University Press, 1985.

Elsen 1985b. Elsen, Albert E. *Rodin's* Thinker *and the Dilemmas of Modern Public Sculpture.* New Haven: Yale University Press, 1985.

Elsen 2003. Elsen, Albert. With Jamison, Rosalyn Frankel. *Rodin's Art: The Rodin Collection, Iris and B. Gerald Cantor Centor for Visual Arts Stanford University*. New York: Oxford University Press, 2003.

Frisch and Shipley 1939. Frisch, Victor, and Shipley, Joseph T. *Auguste Rodin: A Biography*. New York: Frederick Stokes, 1939.

Fusco and Janson 1980. Fusco, Peter, and Janson, H. W., eds. *The Romantics to Rodin: French Nineteenth-Century Sculpture from North American Collections*. Exh. cat., Los Angeles County Museum of Art. New York: George Braziller, 1980.

Geffroy 1886. Geffroy, Gustave. "Chronique—Rodin." *La Justice*, no. 2370 (July 11, 1886).

Geffroy 1889. Geffroy, Gustave. "Auguste Rodin." *Claude Monet–A. Rodin*. Exh. cat. Galerie Georges Petit. Paris: E. Ménard and Cie, 1889, pp. 46–84. Reprinted in Monet-Rodin 1889/1989, pp. 59–68. A somewhat condensed translation appears in Butler 1980, pp. 62–73.

Gsell 1911. Gsell, Paul. *L'art: Entretiens réunis par Paul Gsell / Auguste Rodin*. Paris: Bernard Grasset, 1911. Ed. cit., Paris: L'Imprimerie Aulard, 1951. Republished and translated by Jacques de Caso and Patricia Sanders as *Art: Conversations with Paul Gsell / Auguste Rodin*. Berkeley: University of California Press, 1984.

Gsell 1914. Gsell, Paul. "*Chez Rodin.*" *L'Art et les artistes* 109, special issue *Rodin: L'homme et l'oeuvre* (April 1914), pp. 49–72.

Joliffe 1967. Joliffe, John, ed. and trans. *Froissart's Chronicles*. London: Harvill Press, 1967.

Kahn 1900. Kahn, Gustave. "Les Mains chez Rodin." *La Plume*, special issue *Rodin*, fasc. 1 (May 15, 1900), pp. 12–14. Reprinted in Butler 1980, pp. 106–7.

Kelley 1975. Kelley, David. *Baudelaire: Salon de 1846*. Oxford: Oxford University Press, 1975.

Lampert 1986. Lampert, Catherine. *Rodin: Sculpture and Drawing*. Exh. cat. London: Arts Council of Great Britain, 1986.

Lawton 1906. Lawton, Frederick. *The Life and Work of Auguste Rodin*. London: T. Fisher Unwin, 1906.

Le Normand-Romain 2007. Le Normand-Romain, Antoinette. *The Bronzes of Rodin: Catalogue of Works in the Musée Rodin*. 2 vols. Paris: Éditions de la Réunion des Musées Nationaux, 2007.

Levkoff 1994. Levkoff, Mary. *Rodin in His Time: The Cantor Gifts to the Los Angeles County Museum of Art*. New York: Thames and Hudson, 1994.

McNamara and Elsen 1977. McNamara, Mary Jo, and Elsen, Albert E. *Rodin's Burghers of Calais*. Exh. cat. New York: Cantor Fitzgerald Group, 1977.

Mirbeau 1889. Mirbeau, Octave. "Auguste Rodin." *L'Écho de Paris*, no. 1873 (June 25, 1889), p. 1. Reprinted in Monet-Rodin 1989/1989, p. 226.

Monet-Rodin 1889/1989. *Claude Monet/A. Rodin*. Exh. cat. Galerie Georges Petit. Paris: E. Ménard and Cie, 1889. Facsimile included in *Claude Monet—Auguste Rodin, Centenaire de l'exposition de 1889*. Exh. cat. Paris: Musée Rodin, 1989, pp. 47–69.

Morhardt 1898. Morhardt, Matthias. "Mlle Camille Claudel." *Mercure de France* 25 (March 1898), pp. 709–55.

Newton and MacDonald 1978. Newton, Joy, and MacDonald, Margaret. "Rodin: The Whistler Monument." *Gazette des beaux-arts* 92 (December 1978), pp. 221–32.

Paris and La Chapelle 1990. Paris, Reine-Marie, and La Chapelle, Arnaud de. *L'Oeuvre de Camille Claudel: Catalogue raisonné*. Paris: Adam Biro Editions d'Art et d'Histoire ARHIS, 1990.

Philadelphia 1996. *Rodin and Michelangelo: A Study in Artistic Inspiration*. Exh. cat. Philadelphia Museum of Art (previously Casa Buonarotti, Florence), 1996.

Rilke 1903. Rilke, Rainer Maria. *Rodin*. Berlin: Julius Bard, 1903. Trans. Jessie Lamont and Hans Trausil. New York: Fine Editions Press, 1945. Reprinted in Elsen 1965, pp. 110–44.

Rivère, Gaudichon, and Ghanassia 2000. Rivère, Anne, Gaudichon, Bruno, and Ghanassia, Danielle. *Camille Claudel: Catalogue raisonné, nouvelle edition revue et augmentée*. Paris: Adam Biro, 2000.

Rodin 1914. Rodin, Auguste. *Les Cathedrales de France*. Paris: Armand Colin, 1914. Trans. Elisabeth Chase Geissbuhler. London: Hamlyn Publishing Group, 1965.

Rodin 1985. Rodin, Auguste. *Correspondence de Rodin: I. 1860–1899*. Ed. Alain Beausire and Hélène Pinet. Paris: Éditions du Musée Rodin, 1985.

Ruckstall 1925. Ruckstall, Frederick Wellington. *Great Works of Art and What Makes Them Great*. New York: Putnam, 1925. Republished. Whitefish, Mont.: Kessinger Publishing, 2003.

Steinberg 1972. Steinberg, Leo. "Rodin." *Other Criteria: Confrontations with Twentieth-Century Art*. New York: Oxford University Press, 1972, pp. 322–403. Originally published as the introduction to the exh. cat. *Auguste Rodin, 1840–1917: An Exhibition of Sculptures/ Drawings*. New York: Charles Slatkin Galleries, 1963, pp. 10–27.

Tancock 1967. Tancock, John. "Rodin Is a Rodin Is a Rodin." *Art and Artists* 2, no. 4 (July 1967), pp. 38–41. Reprinted in Butler 1980, pp. 183–87.

Tancock 1976. Tancock, John. *The Sculpture of Auguste Rodin: The Collection of the Rodin Museum, Philadelphia*. Philadelphia: Philadelphia Museum of Art, 1976.

Thoré 1868. Thoré, Théophile [W. Burger]. *Salons de T. Thoré (1844–1848)*. Paris: Librarie Internationale Lacroix, 1868.

Varnedoe 1985. Varnedoe, J. Kirk. "Rodin's Drawings." In Ernst Güse, *Auguste Rodin: Drawings and Watercolors*. New York: Rizzoli, 1985, pp. 13–29.

## PHOTOGRAPHY CREDITS

Unless otherwise acknowledged here, the photographs in this book were taken by staff photographers Karen Malinofski and Christopher Ciccone of the North Carolina Museum of Art. The following photographs appear courtesy of:

Charleville-Mézières, Musée de l'Ardenne et Musée Arthur Rimbaud, FIG. 11A

Copenhagen, Ny Carlsberg Glyptotek, © 2010 Ole Haupt, FIG. 8A

Los Angeles and New York, Los Angeles County Museum of Art/Museum Associates/ Art Resource, FIGS. 10A, 14A, 16B

Los Angeles, Iris and B. Gerald Cantor Foundation, FIGS. 13A, 15A

New York, Metropolitan Museum of Art/Art Resource, FIGS. 9, 10, 6A, 17

Nîmes, Musée des Beaux Arts, FIG. 5

Palo Alto, Stanford University, Iris and B. Gerald Cantor Center for Visual Arts, FIGS. 1; 2; 8; 3A; 14; 4A; 4B; 7B; 16A; 16; 18A; 20A; 21A; 25A; 27A; © 2010 Estate of Albert E. Elsen: FIG. 5B

Paris, Musée Rodin, FIGS. 4; 11; 13; 19; 21; 30A; © 2010 Christian Baraja: FIGS. 1A, 12A, 28A

Paris and New York, Musée du Louvre/Art Resource, FIG. 1C

Paris and New York, Réunion des Musées Nationaux/Art Resource, FIG. 1B

Raleigh, © 2010 Art Howard: FIGS. 12, 5C, 9A, 10B, 13B, 14B, 29A

Raleigh, © 2010 Tom Lopez: FIG. 20

Washington, D.C., Pennell Archives, Library of Congress, FIG. 26A

# INDEX OF WORKS





FSC
Mixed Sources
Cert no. SW-COC-001271
© 1996 FSC